new recipes for your

slo-cooker

new recipes for your

slo-cooker

good food from your slo-cooker

annette yates

foulsham

LONDON • NEW YORK • TORONTO • SYDNEY

foulsham

The Publishing House, Bennetts Close, Cippenham, Slough, Berkshire, SL1 5AP, England

ISBN 0-572-02636-6

Cover photograph by Peter Howard Smith

Printed in Great Britain by St. Edmundsbury Press, Bury St. Edmunds, Suffolk

Contents

Introduction   6

Choosing a Slo-cooker   8

Getting Started   10

Notes on the Recipes   15

Soups, Starters and Sauces   17

Vegetables and Pulses   43

Fish   55

Meat, Poultry and Game   63

Puddings and Desserts   115

And Finally   137

Index   142

Introduction

For those of us who love good food but have little time to spend cooking, slo-cookers can fit perfectly into our busy lifestyles. They can be used day or night, and you don't have to stay in to keep an eye on the pot. Just prepare the ingredients and put them in your slo-cooker before leaving home. Whether you are working, shopping, gardening or exercising at the gym, you can rest assured that a meal is simmering away gently on a low setting, ready to be served up when you get home. And if you happen to be an hour late, you don't have to worry because there is little chance of the food spoiling. In other words, the food will be ready when you are. You can even cook meals overnight for the following day – literally in your sleep!

There are other advantages too. Because a slo-cooker uses only slightly more electricity than a light bulb, you are economising on fuel too, and because the efficient insulation built into the slo-cooker means that only the food inside it heats up and not the whole room – so you won't have to put up with steamy windows and overheated kitchens.

Flavour and quality are also enhanced by the gentle heat of the slo-cooker. There is less evaporation so there is little chance of the food drying out. The steam condenses on the underside of the lid and returns to the pot, sealing in heat, flavour, soluble nutrients and cooking odours. The long cooking time tenderises cheaper, tougher cuts of meat and

mingles flavours to make the best soups, stews and casseroles you have ever tasted. And, perhaps best of all, nothing will ever stick to the bottom of the saucepan.

As an additional benefit, your oven and hob are free for other things – which can be particularly useful when you're cooking for crowds.

I hope you will enjoy trying the recipes in this book as much as I enjoyed creating them. Some are traditional old faithfuls but others are brand new, bringing us up to date with today's ingredients and the way we eat now. I hope too that you will use the recipes as a basis to experiment and develop your own favourite ideas, so that your repertoire of delicious meals, all cooked in your slo-cooker, continues to grow.

Choosing a Slo-cooker

Slo-cookers come in a variety of shapes, sizes and colours. The most popular types have an outer casing made of plastic or metal, plus an inner metal casing and the heating elements are situated between the two. The cooking pot is usually removable for easy washing up, and topped with a well-fitting glass or stoneware lid. Some models consist of a removable metal dish that sits on a heated base, so it heats from the bottom only. These have the advantage of being able to brown meat in the pot and bring the contents to the boil on the hob first. At the time of going to print, they have one heat setting and are available in one size only.

More generally, the heat settings available are LOW (for all-day cooking) and HIGH (for preheating, for cooking foods such as whole poultry and steamed puddings, and for speeding up cooking times). In addition, there is usually an automatic or AUTO function (where cooking starts on HIGH and automatically switches to LOW for the remaining cooking time).

Choose a slo-cooker with a capacity to suit your specific needs and consider whether you will use it for entertaining or for making extra quantities for the freezer. If you regularly cook for only one or two, then a small capacity will be fine, but if you cook for four or more, or if you entertain regularly, a large capacity will suit you better. A large size is also useful if you like to cook in large quantities to freeze for another day.

The shape of the cooking pot is also important. A wide one will be easier to use for foods that need to be cooked in a single layer, such as whole (bell) peppers, fish or fruit. A deep pot will easily accommodate a pudding basin. Your choice will depend on what quantity and type of foods you are likely to cook.

Finally, before buying, do spend a little time looking at the manufacturer's booklet of instructions and recipes, just to check that the slo-cooker is likely to live up to your expectations. Its real forte is cooking dishes that need long, slow, gentle cooking – such as soups, casseroles, pot-roasts and puddings – but, like any other cooking appliance, a slo-cooker cannot do everything.

Getting started

Always read and follow the manufacturer's instructions. This is an obvious statement, I know, but you would be surprised how many people just don't bother.

General hints on using your slo-cooker

- Before starting a recipe, check whether preheating is necessary or not. Preheating is particularly important when using the one-step method (see page 13) and for cooking whole poultry and steamed puddings. Preheating should be done with the lid **on.** While the slo-cooker is heating, prepare the ingredients.

- When you are ready to start cooking, place the ingredients in the slo-cooker. Fill it to a maximum of 2.5 cm/1 in from the top.

- Dishes to be cooked in your slo-cooker must contain some liquid.

- Never leave a slo-cooker containing prepared, uncooked ingredients to be switched on later, and do not store the removable pot in the fridge. If you are not going to start cooking immediately, store prepared ingredients in a separate container in the fridge.

- Put the lid on, select the heat setting and cook for the recommended time. Leave the slo-cooker undisturbed during the cooking period and keep the lid on. If you cannot resist the temptation to lift the lid and peek inside, you will need to add about 30 minutes on to the total cooking time in order to regain the lost heat.

- The cooking time on HIGH is just over half of that on LOW. If you need to speed things up, simply switch to the HIGH setting.

- The LOW setting cooks very gently with hardly any simmering – ideal for casseroles and custard puddings, for instance. The HIGH setting is suitable for foods that can, or need to, simmer and actually boil – for example, the water around steamed puddings.

- Avoid positioning the slo-cooker in direct draughts. If the room is very cold, you may need to allow a slightly longer cooking time, particularly when cooking on LOW.
- If, at the end of the cooking time, the food is not ready, replace the lid, switch to HIGH and continue cooking for a further 30 minutes to 1 hour.
- Once the food is cooked, it can be kept warm if necessary in the slo-cooker on LOW.
- If your slo-cooker has a removable pot, cooked dishes can be browned under the grill (broiler) or covered with a topping and crisped in a preheated oven. Check with your instruction book first.
- Any food left over after serving should be transferred from the slo-cooker, cooled, then chilled or frozen.
- Cooked food should not be reheated in the slo-cooker – it takes too long to reach a temperature that is high enough.

Preparing and using ingredients

Like all cooking methods, slo-cooking demands its own special techniques. To get the best results, follow these guidelines.

- Trim meat of excess fat and cut into even-size cubes.
- Slice vegetables thinly or cut them into small dice. This is necessary because, surprisingly, vegetables take longer to cook than meat in a slo-cooker. I am told that this is because they need to reach a higher temperature in order to begin cooking. If you don't want to cut them too small, place them near the bottom of the pot, below the meat, and make sure they are completely covered with the cooking liquid. Alternatively, you can speed up cooking by softening them in a little oil before adding them to the slo-

cooker, and bringing the cooking liquid to the boil before adding it to the slo-cooker.

- Browning meat and softening vegetables in a little oil on the hob before placing them in the slo-cooker improves the flavour and colour of the finished dish.

- Season food only lightly with salt and pepper. Flavours are sealed in and concentrated in the slo-cooker, so it's best to cook first, then check the seasoning before serving and adjust it if necessary.

- Add thickening agents either at the start or towards the end of cooking. For instance, when softening vegetables or browning meat on the hob, stir in some flour before adding the cooking liquid, bringing to the boil and transferring to the slo-cooker. Alternatively, blend some flour or cornflour with a little water to make a smooth paste and stir it into the

slo-cooker for the last 30 minutes to 1 hour of cooking.

- Always thaw frozen ingredients before placing them in the slo-cooker.

- Frozen vegetables should be thawed first and added to the slo-cooker for the final 30 minutes to 1 hour of cooking time.

- Add pasta and rice to the slo-cooker for the final 30 minutes of the cooking time.

- Cream and milk are best added to savoury dishes during the final 30 minutes cooking, if you add them before they may separate.

Methods of slo-cooking

The browning method

This is my preferred method for cooking meat, poultry and game and produces the best results in terms of colour, texture and, above all, flavour.

- Heat a little oil in a saucepan on the hob and quickly brown the meat on all sides. Transfer to the slo-cooker.
- Add the thinly sliced or diced vegetables to the saucepan and cook for a few minutes.
- Stir into the meat in the slo-cooker.
- Add the remaining ingredients to the saucepan, bring to the boil and pour over the meat and vegetables in the slo-cooker (there should be just enough liquid to cover them).
- Stir some flour into the meat or vegetables before transferring them to the slo-cooker (this will thicken the liquid during cooking). Alternatively, blend some flour or cornflour with a little water and stir into the slo-

cooker for the final 30 minutes to 1 hour of cooking.
- Put the lid on and select the heat setting. Cook for the recommended time.

The one-step method

In this method, the cold ingredients are placed directly into the slo-cooker. Though this is a convenient method when you are especially short of time, the results may not always be as visually impressive as the browning method (see above).

- Preheat the slo-cooker for about 20 minutes while you prepare the ingredients.
- Make sure that vegetables are sliced thinly or cut into fine dice. Place them in the slo-cooker before adding meat or poultry and other ingredients.
- Pour over sufficient boiling liquid (stock, water, wine, cider) to cover.

- If the liquid is to thicken during cooking, blend some flour or cornflour with a little cold water to form a paste and stir in with the rest of the ingredients, or coat the meat, poultry or vegetables with flour before adding them to the slo-cooker. Alternatively, add the thickening during the final 30 minutes to 1 hour of cooking.
- Put the lid on and select the heat setting. Cook for the recommended time, plus 2–3 hours.

Adapting recipes for your slo-cooker

You can adapt your usual, conventional recipes to be cooked in your slo-cooker. Because there is less evaporation in a slo-cooker, you should always reduce the quantity of liquid – use about half the quantity given in your conventional recipe. If the finished result is too thick, you can always add extra boiling stock or other liquid before serving.

Use the table below as a rough guide to cooking times:

Conventional cooking time	Cooking time in a slo-cooker		
	Low	High	Auto
30 minutes	6–8 hours	3–4 hours	5–7 hours
30 minutes–1 hour	8–10 hours	5–6 hours	6–8 hours
1–3 hours	10–12 hours	7–8 hours	8–10 hours

Notes on the Recipes

All the recipes in this book have been tested in a range of slo-cookers. However, slo-cookers vary in their performance from model to model, so it is worth comparing the cooking time of a recipe in this book with a similar one in your own manufacturer's instruction book.

- Measures are given in metric, imperial and American. Follow one set only.
- American terms are given in brackets.
- All spoon measurements are level: 1 tsp = 5 ml; 1 tbsp = 15 ml.
- Eggs are medium unless otherwise stated.

- All herbs are fresh unless dried are specifically called for. If substituting dried herbs for fresh, use half the quantity or less as they are very pungent.
- Always wash, dry, peel and core, if necessary, any fresh produce before use.
- Cooking times are approximate.
- If you alter the quantities of the recipe, the cooking times will vary only slightly.
- Always follow the manufacturer's instructions for your particular slo-cooker.

Soups, Starters and Sauces

The gentle simmering of the slo-cooker is ideal for making all kinds of soups, mingling the flavours together gently while everything cooks at a leisurely pace. Once cooked, the soup can be kept warm and ladled straight from the slo-cooker.

Starters such as pâtés and stuffed vine leaves are ideal for slow cooking and recipes for these are included in the following pages.

You will also find sauces in this section – they can cook gently for hours, ready to accompany pasta, pan-fried (sautéed) fish fillets, grilled (broiled) sausages or chicken, or perhaps barbecued chops, burgers or steaks.

I have started the chapter with a recipe for a well-flavoured home-made stock – the basis of any good soup.

Quick tips for soups and sauces

- Root vegetables take a long time to cook, so cut them into small dice or slice them thinly.
- Soften onions and root vegetables slightly in a little oil in a saucepan on the hob (or in a microwave) before adding to the slo-cooker.
- Brown meat in oil in a saucepan on the hob, before putting it in the slo-cooker, to improve the flavour and colour of the finished soup.

- Use a good-quality stock – it makes all the difference.
- Use about half the stock you would use in a conventional recipe. Unlike hob cooking, little evaporation takes place from the slo-cooker. If, at the end of the cooking period, the soup is too thick, you can always top up with boiling water or extra stock.
- Add seasoning sparingly and adjust it to taste just before serving.
- Add milk or cream to a soup or sauce just 15–30 minutes before serving. If it is added before this there is a danger that it may separate.
- Cooked soup or sauce that has been puréed can be reheated in the slo-cooker for about 30 minutes on HIGH or, to speed things up, in a saucepan on the hob.
- Stir soups before serving.

Home-made stock

About 1.75 kg/4 lb raw or cooked bones or a poultry carcass

1 onion, roughly chopped

2 carrots, roughly chopped

2 celery sticks, roughly chopped

About 10 black peppercorns

A few sprigs of fresh parsley

A few sprigs of fresh thyme

1 bay leaf

There's nothing quite like the flavour of a home-made stock. When slow-cooked, flavours are allowed to develop slowly over many hours on the LOW setting, producing a clear stock (cooking on HIGH will produce a cloudy stock). The best flavour comes from fresh bones that have been browned first – under the grill (broiler) or in a hot oven. I like to freeze stock in small quantities (ice-cube trays are ideal) so that I have it ready to add to a recipe at a moment's notice.

1

Break up the bones as small as possible (to extract the most flavour). Put all the ingredients in the slo-cooker with enough boiling water to cover.

2

Cover and cook on LOW for 10–16 hours.

3

Strain the stock, leave to cool, then chill.

4

Remove any surface fat and chill for up to 2 days or freeze for up to 3 months.

Cooking time
10–16 hours on LOW

Chicken chowder

25 g/1 oz/2 tbsp butter or margarine

1 onion, finely chopped

4 celery sticks, thinly sliced

1 large boneless chicken breast, skinned and cut into small cubes

4 boneless chicken thighs, skinned and cut into small cubes

1 litre/1¾ pts/4¼ cups chicken stock

150 ml/¼ pt/⅔ cup double (heavy) cream

175 g/6 oz/1½ cups drained canned sweetcorn (corn)

Salt and freshly ground black pepper

This is substantial enough to serve as a main dish, with crusty rolls.

Melt the butter or margarine in a saucepan and add the onion, celery and potatoes. Cook for about 5 minutes, stirring occasionally, without browning.

Add the chicken and cook, stirring, for a few minutes until it is no longer pink.

Add the stock, bring just to the boil and pour into the slo-cooker.

Cover and cook on LOW for 7–9 hours, stirring in the cream, sweetcorn and seasoning to taste about 30 minutes before serving.

Cooking time
7–9 hours on LOW

Old-fashioned beef broth

15 ml/1 tbsp oil

225 g/8 oz stewing steak, cut into small pieces

2 onions, finely chopped

1 large carrot, finely chopped

1 potato, about 225 g/8 oz, cut into small dice

1 leek, thinly sliced

15 ml/1 tbsp plain (all-purpose) flour

1.2 litres/2 pts/5 cups beef stock

30 ml/2 tbsp pearl barley

Salt and freshly ground black pepper

30 ml/2 tbsp chopped fresh parsley

For Chicken Broth, follow this recipe, replacing the beef with chicken meat and the beef stock with chicken stock.

1

Heat the oil in a frying pan (skillet) and cook the steak, stirring occasionally, until brown. Transfer to the slo-cooker.

2

Add the vegetables to the saucepan and cook for about 5 minutes without browning, stirring occasionally.

3

Stir the flour into the vegetables, then gradually stir in the stock. Add the pearl barley and seasoning and bring just to the boil. Pour into the slo-cooker and stir well.

4

Cover and cook on LOW for 6–10 hours.

5

Stir well and adjust seasoning to taste. Just before serving, stir in the parsley.

Cooking time
6–10 hours on LOW

Butter bean and tomato soup SERVES 4–6

30 ml/2 tbsp olive oil

1 onion, finely chopped

2 carrots, finely chopped

2 celery sticks, thinly sliced

225 g/8 oz/1⅓ cups dried butter (fava) beans, soaked in plenty of cold water overnight and drained

400 g/14 oz/1 large can of chopped tomatoes

1 litre/1¾ pts/4¼ cups vegetable stock

10 ml/2 tsp dried mixed herbs

Salt and freshly ground black pepper

Chopped fresh parsley, to serve

Scatter small, crisp bacon pieces over the surface of each bowl of soup, if liked, and serve with garlic bread.

Heat the oil in a large saucepan and add the onion, carrots and celery. Cook for about 5 minutes, stirring occasionally, without browning.

Add the remaining ingredients, except for the parsley, bring to the boil and transfer to the slo-cooker.

Cover and cook on HIGH for 6–9 hours (the cooking time will depend on the age of the butter beans, older ones will take longer).

Stir well and adjust seasoning to taste. Add some parsley just before serving.

Cooking time
6–9 hours on HIGH

Split pea soup

30 ml/2 tbsp oil

2 lean streaky bacon rashers (slices), rinded and finely chopped

1 leek, thinly sliced

1 celery stick, finely chopped

225 g/8 oz/1⅓ cups split dried green peas, soaked overnight in plenty of cold water

1 litre/1¾ pts/4¼ cups ham or chicken stock

2.5 ml/½ tsp dried mixed herbs

Salt and freshly ground black pepper

60 ml/4 tbsp double (heavy) cream or crème fraîche (optional)

Slow cooking is ideal for ingredients that need long cooking time, such as dried peas and beans, but don't forget that pulses must be soaked overnight in cold water before cooking. Leave the soup to cook all day (or all night) and make the finishing touches just before serving.

1

In a large saucepan, heat the oil and cook the bacon, leek and celery for about 5 minutes, stirring occasionally.

2

Add the drained peas, stock, herbs and a little seasoning. Bring just to the boil, then transfer to the slo-cooker.

3

Cover and cook on LOW for 8–12 hours.

4

To make a chunky soup, use a potato masher to mash up the peas and thicken the soup. To make a smooth soup, tip into a processor or blender and purée until smooth.

5

Just before serving, stir in the cream or crème fraîche, if using.

Cooking time
8–12 hours on LOW

French onion soup

30 ml/2 tbsp olive oil

700 g/1½ lb onions, thinly sliced

10 ml/2 tsp sugar

30 ml/2 tbsp cornflour (cornstarch)

1 litre/1¾ pts/4¼ cups beef or
   chicken stock

1–2 bay leaves (optional)

Salt and freshly ground black
   pepper

6 slices of French bread

75 g/3 oz/¾ cup grated Gruyère
   (Swiss) or Cheddar cheese

This recipe can be adapted to make Cream of Onion Soup. At the end of step 3, tip the soup into a processor or blender and purée until smooth. Stir in 150 ml/½ pt/ ⅔ cup double (heavy) cream and reheat. Scatter some chopped fresh parsley on top of each serving.

1

Heat the oil in a frying pan (skillet), add the onions and sugar and cook gently for about 15 minutes, stirring occasionally until soft and golden brown.

2

Stir in the cornflour, then gradually stir in the stock. Add the bay leaves, if using, and season with a little salt and pepper. Bring just to the boil, then transfer to the slo-cooker.

3

Cover and cook on LOW for 6–8 hours. Discard the bay leaves before serving.

4

Pile the cheese on to the slices of bread and put under a hot grill (broiler) until bubbling and golden brown.

5

Either place a slice in the bottom of each serving bowl before ladling the soup over the top, or float a slice on the surface of each serving.

Cooking time
6–8 hours on LOW

Spiced lentil and coconut soup

30 ml/2 tbsp olive oil

1 red onion, finely chopped

1 garlic clove, crushed

1 carrot, finely chopped

5 ml/1 tsp ground cumin

5 ml/1 tsp ground coriander
(cilantro)

175 g/6 oz/1 cup red lentils

1 litre/1¾ pts/4¼ cups vegetable
stock

Salt and freshly ground black
pepper

2 leeks, thinly sliced

200 ml/7 fl oz/1 carton of coconut
cream

Chopped fresh coriander (cilantro),
to serve

This is very good served with warm naan bread.

1

Heat the oil in a large saucepan and add the onion, garlic and carrot. Cook for about 3 minutes, stirring occasionally, without browning.

2

Add the spices and cook, stirring for 2–3 minutes.

3

Stir in the lentils, stock and seasoning, bring to the boil and pour into the slo-cooker. Stir in the sliced leeks.

4

Cover and cook on LOW for 5–7 hours, adding the coconut cream for the final 30 minutes.

5

Just before serving, adjust seasoning to taste and stir in some chopped fresh coriander.

Cooking time
5–7 hours on LOW

Fresh tomato soup

30 ml/2 tbsp olive oil

1 onion, finely chopped

1 garlic clove, crushed

1 carrot, finely chopped

700 g/1½ lb ripe tomatoes, skinned and chopped

900 ml/1½ pts/3¾ cups chicken or vegetable stock

30 ml/2 tbsp tomato purée (paste)

15 ml/1 tbsp sugar, plus extra to taste

10 ml/2 tsp chopped fresh oregano

Salt and freshly ground black pepper

30 ml/2 tbsp finely chopped fresh herbs, such as basil, oregano, thyme or parsley

If you prefer a smooth soup, simply tip the cooked mixture into a processor or blender and purée. For Cream of Tomato Soup, add 150 ml/¼ pt/⅔ cup double (heavy) cream at step 4, then reheat before adding the herbs and sugar. Sugar is an important seasoning in this recipe, so don't be afraid to add extra to taste.

1

Heat the oil in a large saucepan and cook the onion, garlic and carrot for about 5 minutes, stirring occasionally.

2

Stir in all the remaining ingredients, except the fresh herbs, and bring just to the boil. Transfer to the slo-cooker.

3

Cover and cook on LOW for 8–10 hours.

4

Add extra sugar and seasoning to taste and stir in the fresh herbs just before serving.

Cooking time
8–10 hours on LOW

Red lentil soup

30 ml/2 tbsp oil

4 lean bacon rashers (slices), rinded and finely chopped

1 large onion, finely chopped

2 carrots, finely chopped

1.2 litre/2 pts/5 cups ham, chicken or vegetable stock

25 ml/1½ tbsp tomato purée (paste)

225 g/8 oz/1⅓ cups red lentils

Serve this filling soup with chunks of crusty bread. I like to scatter some crisp-cooked bacon strips over each serving.

1

Heat the oil in a frying pan (skillet) and cook the bacon, onion and carrots for 5–10 minutes, stirring occasionally, until just beginning to turn golden brown.

2

Stir in the remaining ingredients and bring just to the boil. Transfer to the slo-cooker.

3

Cover and cook on LOW for 6–8 hours.

4

Tip into a processor or blender and purée until smooth. Reheat and serve.

Cooking time
6–8 hours on LOW

Winter vegetable soup

25 g/1 oz/2 tbsp butter or margarine

15 ml/1 tbsp olive oil

2 onions, finely chopped

1 large carrot, cut into small dice

1 parsnip, cut into small dice

2 celery sticks, finely chopped

225 g/8 oz tomatoes, skinned and chopped

30 ml/2 tbsp plain (all-purpose) flour

1 litre/1¾ pts/4¼ cups vegetable stock

10 ml/2 tsp chopped fresh mint

15 ml/1 tbsp wholegrain mustard

Salt and freshly ground black pepper

Chopped fresh herbs, to garnish

This recipe uses root vegetables as its base. Use your favourites – or for a change, add celeriac (celery root) or use fennel in place of celery.

1

Heat the butter or margarine and oil in a large saucepan and add the onions, carrot, parsnip and celery. Cook, stirring occasionally, for 5–10 minutes until soft and just beginning to turn golden brown.

2

Add the tomatoes and stir in the flour. Gradually stir in the stock, then add the mint, mustard and seasoning.

3

Bring just to the boil, then transfer to the slo-cooker.

4

Cover and cook on LOW for 6–10 hours.

5

Stir well and adjust seasoning to taste before serving, garnished with fresh herbs.

Cooking time
6–10 hours on LOW

Watercress soup

25 g/1 oz/2 tbsp butter or
 margarine

1 onion, finely chopped

1 garlic clove, crushed

1 potato, thinly sliced

2 bunches of watercress, roughly
 chopped

600 ml/1 pt/2½ cups chicken stock

Salt and freshly ground black
 pepper

300 ml/½ pt/1⅓ cups milk

I serve this light soup as a starter at supper parties.

Heat the butter or margarine in a large saucepan and cook the onion and garlic for about 5 minutes, stirring occasionally, without browning.

Add the potato and watercress and cook, stirring, for a further 2–3 minutes.

Add the stock and a little seasoning and bring just to the boil. Transfer to the slo-cooker.

Cover and cook on LOW for 6–8 hours.

Tip the soup into a processor or blender and purée until smooth. Stir in the milk and reheat before serving, adjusting the seasoning to taste.

Cooking time
6–8 hours on LOW

Vichyssoise

25 g/1 oz/2 tbsp butter or margarine

1 onion, finely chopped

1 garlic clove, crushed (optional)

700 g/1½ lb leeks (white parts only), thinly sliced

1 large potato, cut into small dice

900 ml/1½ pts/3¾ cups chicken or vegetable stock

Salt and freshly ground black pepper

150 ml/¼ pt/⅔ cup double (heavy) cream

Snipped fresh chives, to serve

Traditionally this pale, delicate soup is served cold. For Leek and Potato Soup, make up the recipe using both green and white parts of the leeks, and serve hot.

1

Heat the butter or margarine in a large saucepan and cook the onion, garlic and leeks gently for about 10 minutes, stirring occasionally, without browning.

2

Add the potato and stock and season with a little salt and pepper. Bring just to the boil, then transfer to the slo-cooker.

3

Cook on LOW for 8–10 hours.

4

Tip the soup into a processor or blender and purée until smooth. Cool and chill.

5

Serve chilled, with the cream stirred in and sprinkled with snipped fresh chives.

Cooking time
8–10 hours on LOW

Chilled cucumber and mint soup

30 ml/2 tbsp olive oil

1 onion, finely chopped

1 large cucumber, peeled and sliced

600 ml/1 pt/2½ cups chicken or
    vegetable stock

30–45 ml/2–3 tbsp finely chopped
    mint leaves, plus extra to serve

5 ml/1 tsp sugar

Salt and freshly ground black
    pepper

250 ml/8 fl oz/1 cup milk

150 ml/¼ pt/⅔ cup plain yoghurt or
    crème fraîche, plus extra to
    serve

This summer soup is delicious served with crisp croûtons or Melba toast.

1

Heat the oil in a large saucepan and cook the onion for about 5 minutes without browning.

2

Stir in the cucumber, stock, mint, sugar and a little salt and pepper. Bring just to the boil, then transfer to the slo-cooker.

3

Cover and cook on LOW for 4–8 hours.

4

Tip the soup into a processor or blender and purée until smooth. Stir in the milk and yoghurt or crème fraîche, cool and chill.

5

Adjust seasoning to taste. Serve in chilled bowls topped with a little extra yoghurt or crème fraîche and some chopped mint.

Cooking time
4–8 hours on LOW

Traditional mulligatawny soup

50 g/2 oz/¼ cup butter or margarine

1 large onion, very thinly sliced

1 garlic clove, crushed

1 carrot, cut into small dice

1 celery stick, very thinly sliced

15 ml/1 tbsp curry powder

30 ml/2 tbsp plain (all-purpose) flour

1.2 litre/2 pts/5 cups chicken stock

1 large cooking (tart) apple, peeled, cored and cut into small dice

10 ml/2 tsp lemon juice

30 ml/2 tbsp basmati or other long-grain rice

2 boneless chicken thighs, skinned and cut into small pieces

Salt and ground black pepper

45 ml/3 tbsp single(light) cream

30 ml/2 tbsp chopped fresh coriander (cilantro)

Make this soup as spicy as you like. It's good served with naan bread.

1

Heat the butter or margarine in a large saucepan and add the onion, garlic, carrot and celery. Cook for about 5 minutes, stirring occasionally, without browning.

2

Add the curry powder and cook for about 2 minutes, stirring.

3

Stir in the flour, then gradually stir in the stock. Add the apple, lemon juice, rice, chicken and a little seasoning. Bring just to the boil, then transfer to the slo-cooker.

4

Cover and cook on LOW for 7–9 hours.

5

Just before serving, remove the pot from the slo-cooker and stir in the cream and coriander.

Cooking time
7–9 hours on LOW

Farmhouse pâté

25 g/1 oz/2 tbsp butter or margarine

4 streaky bacon rashers (slices), rinded

1 onion, finely chopped

225 g/8 oz chicken livers

225 g/8 oz lambs' liver, sliced

225 g/8 oz belly pork, minced (ground)

1 garlic clove, crushed

1 egg, beaten

30 ml/2 tbsp double (heavy) cream

5 ml/1 tsp mustard powder

15 ml/1 tbsp finely chopped fresh sage

Salt and freshly ground black pepper

Crusty bread, to serve

1
Preheat the slo-cooker on HIGH for 20 minutes.

2
Grease a 15 cm/6 in cake tin (pan) with a little of the butter or margarine. Using the back of a knife, stretch the bacon rashers, then use them to line the prepared tin, leaving the edges hanging over the sides.

3
Melt the remaining butter or margarine in a frying pan (skillet) and cook the onion for about 5 minutes, stirring occasionally, until softened but not browned. Add the chicken and lambs' livers and cook, stirring, for 1–2 minutes.

4
Mince the mixture or purée it in a processor, then mix it with the remaining ingredients. Spoon the mixture into the prepared container, pressing down lightly and folding the ends of the bacon over the top. Cover with foil.

5
Put the container in the slo-cooker and add sufficient boiling water to come halfway up its sides. Cover and cook on HIGH for 3–4 hours.

6
Lift the tin out of the slo-cooker and place a weight on the top while the pâté cools. Chill, then serve with lots of crusty bread.

Cooking time
3–4 hours on HIGH

Chicken liver pâté

4 streaky bacon rashers (slices), rinded

450 g/1 lb chicken livers

1 onion, thinly sliced

2 cloves

2 bay leaves

1 bouquet garni (sachet)

Salt and freshly ground black pepper

1 garlic clove, crushed

50 g/2 oz/¼ cup butter or margarine

50 g/2 oz/½ cup plain (all-purpose) flour

150 ml/¼ pt/⅔ cup milk

30 ml/2 tbsp double (heavy) cream

1 egg

Melba toast or crusty bread, to serve

1 Preheat the slo-cooker on HIGH for 20 minutes.

2 Using the back of a knife, stretch the bacon rashers and lay them across the base of an ovenproof pâté dish.

3 Put the livers, onion, cloves, bay leaves, bouquet garni and a pinch of salt in a saucepan and just cover with water. Simmer for a few minutes until the livers stiffen. Leave to cool.

4 Discard the cloves, bay leaves and bouquet garni. Put the livers, onion, garlic and 30 ml/2 tbsp of the cooking liquid into a food processor and purée until smooth.

5 Heat the butter or margarine in a saucepan, stir in the flour and cook, stirring, for 1 minute. Gradually stir in the milk, then bring to the boil and simmer for 2 minutes, stirring continuously.

6 Remove from the heat and add the liver mixture, cream and egg. Season lightly with salt and pepper.

7 Spoon the mixture into the prepared dish, cover with foil and place in the preheated slo-cooker. Add sufficient boiling water to come halfway up the dish.

8 Cover and cook on HIGH for 5–7 hours.

9

Lift the dish out of the slo-cooker, leave to cool, then chill until ready to serve with Melba toast or crusty bread.

Cooking time
5–7 hours on HIGH

Stuffed vine leaves

225 g/8 oz/1 cup long-grain rice

30 ml/2 tbsp olive oil

1 onion, finely chopped

30 ml/2 tbsp pine nuts

2 large tomatoes, finely chopped

30 ml/2 tbsp chopped fresh parsley

30 ml/2 tbsp chopped fresh mint

2.5 ml/½ tsp ground cinnamon

Salt and freshly ground black
pepper

225 g/8 oz vine leaves, fresh or
packed in brine

2 garlic cloves, cut into slivers

Juice of 1 lemon

45 ml/3 tbsp dry white wine

Serve these warm, cold or at room temperature, as a starter or as part of a selection of dishes.

1

Cook the rice according to the packet instructions, then drain, rinse in cold water and drain again. Tip into a large bowl.

2

Heat 15 ml/1 tbsp oil in a small saucepan, add the onion and pine nuts and cook for about 5 minutes, stirring occasionally, until softened and golden brown. Add to the rice with the tomatoes, herbs, cinnamon and seasonings and mix well.

3

Take a vine leaf, veins uppermost, and top with a small spoonful of the rice mixture. Roll up securely into a fat cigar shape and place in the slo-cooker. Repeat with the remaining vine leaves and rice mixture, packing the rolls tightly into the slo-cooker and pressing them down gently.

4

Tuck the garlic slivers between the rolls. Pour over 150 ml/¼ pt/⅔ cup water, then drizzle over the remaining oil, the lemon juice and white wine.

5

Cover and cook on AUTO for about 4 hours until tender and all the liquid has been absorbed. Lift the slo-cooker pot from its base and cool.

Cooking time
about 4 hours on AUTO

Spanish sauce

25 g/1 oz/2 tbsp butter or
margarine

2 lean streaky bacon rashers
(slices), rinded and finely
chopped

1 onion, finely chopped

1 carrot, finely chopped

50 g/2 oz/½ cup closed-cup
mushrooms, chopped

60 ml/4 tbsp plain (all-purpose)
flour

900 ml/1½ pts/3¾ cups beef stock

45 ml/3 tbsp tomato purée (paste)

1 bouquet garni (sachet)

Salt and freshly ground black
pepper

*This is based on a classic French sauce that is
particularly good served with red meats and game.*

1

Heat the butter or margarine in a saucepan and
add the bacon, onion, carrot and mushrooms. Cook
for about 8 minutes, stirring occasionally, without
browning.

2

Stir in the flour, then gradually stir in the stock
and tomato purée. Add the bouquet garni and
season with a little salt and pepper. Bring to the
boil, stirring, then transfer to the slo-cooker.

3

Cover and cook on LOW for 5–7 hours.

4

Stir well before serving.

Cooking time
5–7 hours on LOW

Curry sauce

15 ml/1 tbsp oil

450 g/1 lb onions, finely chopped

10 ml/2 tsp sugar

30 ml/2 tbsp curry paste

45 ml/3 tbsp plain (all-purpose) flour

600 ml/1 pt/2½ cups chicken or vegetable stock

200 g/7 oz/1 small can of chopped tomatoes

30 ml/2 tbsp wine vinegar or lemon juice

30 ml/2 tbsp mango chutney, finely chopped

Salt and freshly ground black pepper

This is delicious with grilled (broiled) meat and fish or roasted vegetables. Adjust the amount of curry paste to suit your taste.

❶

Heat the oil in a large saucepan and add the onions and sugar. Cover and cook over a low heat, stirring occasionally, for about 10 minutes, until very soft and golden brown.

❷

Add the curry paste and cook, stirring, for 2 minutes.

❸

Stir in the flour, then gradually stir in the stock. Add the tomatoes, vinegar and chutney.

❹

Bring to the boil stirring, season lightly and transfer to the slo-cooker.

❺

Cover and cook on LOW for 6–8 hours.

❻

Stir well before serving.

Cooking time
6–8 hours on LOW

Sweet and sour sauce

15 ml/1 tbsp oil

1 onion, finely chopped

1 garlic clove, crushed

30 ml/2 tbsp cornflour (cornstarch)

150 ml/¼ pt/⅔ cup dry sherry

60 ml/4 tbsp soy sauce

30 ml/2 tbsp wine or rice vinegar

300 ml/½ pt/1¼ cups chicken or
    vegetable stock

250 g/9 oz/1 medium can of
    crushed pineapple

30 ml/2 tbsp soft brown sugar

Salt and freshly ground black
    pepper

*Try this with grilled (broiled) or barbecued sausages or
chicken or pork chops.*

1

Heat the oil in a saucepan and cook the onion and garlic for about 5 minutes, stirring occasionally, without browning.

2

Stir in the cornflour, then gradually stir in the sherry, soy sauce, vinegar and stock. Add the pineapple, sugar and seasonings.

3

Bring to the boil, stirring, then transfer to the slo-cooker.

4

Cover and cook on LOW for 4–6 hours.

5

Stir well before serving.

Cooking time
4–6 hours on LOW

Mushroom sauce

15 ml/1 tbsp olive oil

15 g/½ oz/1 tbsp butter or margarine

1 onion, finely chopped

1 garlic clove, crushed (optional)

30 ml/2 tbsp cornflour (cornstarch)

300 ml/½ pt/1¼ cups beef, chicken or vegetable stock

700 g/1½ lb mushrooms, sliced

30 ml/2 tbsp Worcestershire sauce

30 ml/2 tbsp tomato purée (paste)

10 ml/2 tsp chopped fresh oregano or mint

Salt and freshly ground black pepper

Serve with fish, chicken or pasta. As a delicious variation, try adding 150 ml/¼ pt/⅔ cup soured (dairy sour) cream and 30 ml/2 tbsp snipped chives about 30 minutes before serving.

Heat the oil and butter or margarine in a large saucepan and cook the onion and garlic, if using, for about 5 minutes, stirring occasionally, without browning.

Stir in the cornflour, then gradually stir in the stock. Add the remaining ingredients and bring to the boil. Transfer to the slo-cooker.

Cover and cook on LOW for 4–8 hours.

Stir well before serving.

Cooking time
4–8 hours on LOW

Fresh tomato sauce

30 ml/2 tbsp olive oil

1 onion, finely chopped

1 small carrot, finely chopped

1 celery stick, finely chopped

4 lean streaky bacon rashers (slices), rinded and finely chopped

30 ml/2 tbsp plain (all-purpose) flour

600 ml/1 pt/2½ cups chicken or vegetable stock

450 g/1 lb ripe tomatoes, skinned and chopped

5 ml/2 tsp sugar

5 ml/1 tsp oregano, or 15 ml/ 1 tbsp chopped fresh oregano

A pinch of ground cloves (optional)

Salt and freshly ground black pepper

For Chilli Tomato Sauce, omit the cloves and add 5 ml/1 tsp or more of hot chilli sauce.

Heat the oil in a large saucepan and add the onion, carrot, celery and bacon. Cook for about 10 minutes, stirring occasionally, until just beginning to turn golden brown.

Stir in the flour, then gradually stir in the stock. Add the remaining ingredients and bring to the boil. Transfer to the slo-cooker.

Cover and cook on LOW for 7–10 hours.

Stir well. It may be left as it is – chunky – or puréed until smooth in a processor or blender before serving, as you prefer.

Cooking time
7–10 hours on LOW

Vegetables and Pulses

Vegetables cooked in a slo-cooker stay beautifully whole, but they still taste delicious even when they are cooked until very soft. All types of casserole-type dishes with root vegetables and pulses work extremely well, as do vegetable dishes that normally require long, gentle simmering, such as Ratatouille (see page 50).

On occasions when I have a house full of guests, my slo-cooker is really useful for cooking an extra vegetable dish and freeing up hob space.

Quick tips for fresh and frozen vegetables

- Fresh vegetables take much longer to cook in the slo-cooker than they do on the hob. Cut them into small even pieces or slice them thinly. Vegetables such as onions, carrots, swede/rutabaga and potatoes take the longest to cook.

- Avoid cooking vegetables and vegetable recipes from cold. It's always better to bring them to the boil on the hob first, so that they quickly reach a temperature where they can begin to cook. Immersing the vegetables in hot liquid produces the best results.

- Fresh vegetables are best cooked as part of a recipe – it's not a good idea to try and cook them singly in water as you would on the hob.

- Speed up cooking by first softening vegetables in a little oil in a saucepan on the hob (alternatively, use a microwave).

- Thaw frozen vegetables before adding them to the hot slo-cooker, to prevent the temperature plunging in the pot.
- Cooked vegetables can be added to a hot slo-cooker dish 30 minutes to 1 hour before the end of cooking time.
- Be wary of adding too much salt and pepper – it's easy to over-season vegetables and they can dry out. I prefer to adjust the seasoning to taste just before serving.
- Add milk or cream to a recipe for the final 30 minutes cooking only.

Quick tips for pulses

- Canned varieties of beans, peas and lentils are ideal for using in the slo-cooker.
- Dried beans and peas need soaking overnight in plenty of cold water before use. Once soaked, drain them and bring to the boil (either in fresh water or with other recipe ingredients) before adding to the slo-cooker. Dried red kidney beans MUST be boiled rapidly for 10–15 minutes to destroy natural toxins before adding to the slo-cooker.
- Red lentils need no soaking. Simply bring them to the boil before adding to the slo- cooker.
- Immersing the pulses in hot liquid produces the best results.
- Season after cooking or the salt will toughen the pulses and lengthen the cooking time considerably.

Courgettes in apple juice

40 g/1½ oz/3 tbsp butter or margarine

450 g/1 lb courgettes (zucchini), cut into 2.5 cm/1 in lengths

1 garlic clove, crushed

1 small onion, finely chopped

15 ml/1 tbsp cornflour (cornstarch)

300 ml/½ pt/1¼ cups dry apple juice

Salt and freshly ground black pepper

4 fresh tomatoes, skinned and sliced

4 sun-dried tomatoes, chopped (optional)

Serve this as an accompaniment to grilled (broiled) sausages, chops or fish. Alternatively, serve it with crusty bread as a snack or light lunch, topped with grated cheese.

1

Heat the butter or margarine in a frying pan (skillet) and quickly cook the courgettes until lightly browned. Transfer to the slo-cooker.

2

Add the garlic and onion to the saucepan and cook for 3–5 minutes, stirring occasionally, without browning.

3

Stir in the cornflour, then gradually stir in the apple juice. Season lightly with salt and pepper and add the fresh tomatoes and the sun-dried tomatoes, if using. Bring just to the boil, stirring continuously. Pour the sauce over the courgettes in the slo-cooker.

4

Cover and cook on LOW for 4–5 hours.

5

Stir gently before serving and adjust the seasoning to taste.

Cooking time
4–5 hours on LOW

Winter vegetables in coconut cream

550 g/1¼ lb peeled celeriac (celery root), cut into cubes

2 carrots, thinly sliced

2 small parsnips, thinly sliced

30 ml/2 tbsp olive oil

1 large onion, thinly sliced

2 garlic cloves, crushed

30 ml/2 tbsp finely chopped fresh root ginger

15 ml/1 tbsp curry paste

5 ml/1 tsp ground turmeric

2.5 ml/½ tsp crushed chilli

Salt and freshly ground black pepper

300 ml/½ pt/1¼ cups vegetable stock

200 ml/7 fl oz/scant 1 cup coconut cream

Chopped fresh coriander (cilantro), to serve

The vegetables stay beautifully whole and retain a certain 'bite' that contrasts well with the creamy sauce. Serve it with freshly cooked rice and plenty of chopped fresh coriander (cilantro).

1

Put the celeriac, carrots and parsnips into the slo-cooker.

2

Heat the oil in a large saucepan and add the onion, garlic and ginger. Cook for about 5 minutes, stirring occasionally, without browning.

3

Stir the curry paste, turmeric, chilli and seasoning into the saucepan. Add the stock, bring just to the boil and pour over the vegetables in the slo-cooker, coating them completely.

4

Cover and cook on LOW for 6–8 hours, adding the coconut cream for the final 30 minutes.

5

Just before serving, add fresh coriander to taste.

Cooking time
6–8 hours on LOW

Greek mushrooms

30 ml/2 tbsp olive oil

1 onion, finely chopped

2 garlic cloves, crushed

450 g/1 lb button mushrooms

225 g/8 oz chestnut mushrooms

400 g/14 oz/1 large can of
   tomatoes

15 ml/1 tbsp fresh thyme leaves

Salt and freshly ground black
   pepper

15 ml/1 tbsp chopped fresh parsley

Serve these on hot buttered toast or to accompany grilled (broiled) steak or fish.

Heat the oil in a saucepan and cook the onion and garlic for about 5 minutes, stirring occasionally, without browning.

Add the mushrooms, tomatoes and thyme and season with salt and pepper. Bring just to the boil and transfer to the slo-cooker.

Cover and cook on LOW for 2–3 hours.

Stir in the parsley and adjust the seasoning to taste before serving.

Cooking time
2–3 hours on LOW

Curried chickpeas and okra

30 ml/2 tbsp oil

1 onion, thinly sliced

2 garlic cloves, crushed

350 g/12 oz carrots, thinly sliced

225 g/8 oz sweet potatoes, cut into cubes

225 g/8 oz waxy or salad potatoes, cut into cubes

60 ml/4 tbsp curry paste

400 g/14 oz/1 large can of chickpeas (garbanzos), drained

600 ml/1 pt/2½ cups vegetable stock

Salt

50 g/2 oz/⅓ cup red lentils

100 g/4 oz okra (lady's fingers), halved crossways

400 g/14 oz/1 large can of cherry tomatoes

Using curry paste instead of individual spices makes this quick and easy to prepare. Lentils and okra help to thicken the sauce, while the cherry tomatoes stay beautifully whole. Serve it with basmati rice.

1

Heat the oil in a large saucepan and add the onion, garlic and carrots. Cook for about 5 minutes, stirring occasionally, without browning.

2

Stir in the potatoes, curry paste, chickpeas and stock and season with a little salt. Bring to the boil and transfer to the slo-cooker.

3

Stir in the lentils and okra and, finally, gently stir in the tomatoes.

4

Cover and cook on LOW for 7–9 hours.

5

Stir gently and adjust seasoning to taste before serving.

Cooking time
7–9 hours on LOW

Above **Vichyssoise**
(*page 30*)

Right **Fresh Tomato Soup**
(*page 26*)

Above **French Onion Soup** *(page 24)*

Right **Winter Vegetable Soup** *(page 28)*

Below **Chicken Liver Pâté** *(page 34)*

Cheese-stuffed onions

4 onions

100 g/4 oz/1 cup grated Cheddar
cheese

50 g/2 oz/1 cup fresh breadcrumbs

15 ml/1 tbsp chopped fresh herbs,
such as parsley, sage or thyme

Salt and freshly ground black
pepper

150 ml/¼ pt/⅔ cup hot vegetable
stock

*Serve these stuffed onions as a side dish or as a main
course with salad.*

Peel the onions and cut the bases flat so that
they stand upright. Place in a saucepan, cover with
water, bring to the boil, then simmer for 3 minutes.
Drain well and, with a knife or spoon, remove the
cores. You can use the cores for another recipe, or
chop them and add them to the stuffing in step 2.

Combine the cheese, breadcrumbs and herbs
and season well with salt and pepper. Mix in the
chopped onion cores, if using. Spoon the mixture
into the onion centres, pressing down firmly. Stand
the onions in the slo-cooker and pour gently over
the hot stock.

Cover and cook on LOW for 6–8 hours.

Cooking time
6–8 hours on LOW

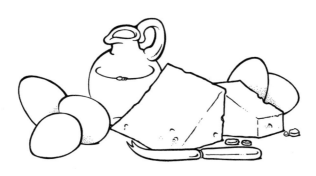

Ratatouille

6 tbsp olive oil

1 large onion, thinly sliced

2 garlic cloves, crushed

1 yellow (bell) pepper, thinly sliced

1 red (bell) pepper, thinly sliced

1 large aubergine (eggplant), cut
   into small cubes

3 courgettes (zucchini), thickly
   sliced

450 g/1 lb tomatoes, skinned,
   seeded and chopped
   OR 400 g/14 oz/1 large can of
   chopped tomatoes

30 ml/2 tbsp tomato purée (paste)

Salt and freshly ground black
   pepper

30 ml/2 tbsp fresh thyme or
   oregano leaves

15 ml/1 tbsp chopped fresh parsley

Serve hot or at room temperature, as a starter or as a main course. Try topping it with a little grated cheese and serving with garlic bread.

Heat the oil in a large saucepan and cook the onion, garlic and peppers for about 5 minutes, stirring occasionally, without browning.

Add all the remaining ingredients, except the parsley. Heat through, turning the vegetables and mixing them thoroughly, until just bubbling. Transfer to the slo-cooker.

Cover and cook on LOW for 5–8 hours.

Stir in the parsley before serving.

Cooking time
5–8 hours on LOW

Leek and cider hot-pot

40 g/1½ oz/3 tbsp butter or margarine

100 g/4 oz lean bacon, rinded and chopped

900 g/2 lb leeks, sliced

2 eating (dessert) apples, peeled, cored and sliced

3 tbsp plain (all-purpose) flour

300 ml/½ pt/1¼ cups dry cider or perry

300 ml/½ pt/1¼ cups vegetable stock

Salt and freshly ground black pepper

Serve as a side dish or main course with garlic bread or freshly cooked rice.

1

Heat the butter or margarine in a large saucepan and cook the bacon for about 5 minutes, stirring occasionally, until golden brown. Stir in the leeks and apples and toss together well.

2

Add the flour, mix well, then gradually stir in the cider and stock. Bring to the boil, stirring continuously. Transfer to the slo-cooker.

3

Cover and cook on LOW for 6–8 hours.

4

Stir and adjust seasoning to taste before serving.

Cooking time
6–8 hours on LOW

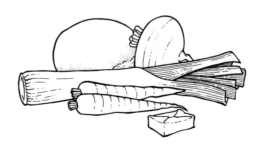

Persian rice

15 ml/1 tbsp olive oil

1 onion, finely chopped

225 g/8 oz/1 cup basmati rice

1 red (bell) pepper, chopped

175 g/6 oz/1½ cups toasted nuts

50 g/2 oz/⅓ cup raisins or chopped
  dried apricots

300 ml/½ pt/1¼ cups vegetable
  stock

5 ml/1 tsp ground mixed (apple-
  pie) spice

Salt and freshly ground black
  pepper

*A pretty dish that can be served hot or at room
temperature as a main course with salads or as a side
dish. It goes particularly well with grilled (broiled) fish or
meat. Use a mixture of walnut pieces, flaked almonds
and pine nuts.*

1

Heat the oil in a large saucepan and cook the
onion for about 5 minutes, stirring occasionally,
without browning.

2

Add the rice and cook for 2 minutes, stirring.

3

Stir in the remaining ingredients, seasoning
lightly with salt and pepper. Transfer to the slo-
cooker.

4

Cover and cook on LOW for 5–7 hours.

Cooking time
5–7 hours on LOW

Spiced vegetables and barley

425 g/15 oz/1 large can of chickpeas (garbanzos), drained

410 g/14 oz/1 large can of red kidney beans, drained

200 g/7 oz/1 small can of chopped tomatoes

50 g/2 oz/⅓ cup pearl barley

2 carrots, cut into small dice

2 parsnips, cut into small dice

30 ml/2 tbsp olive oil

1 large onion, thinly sliced

1 garlic clove, crushed

5 ml/1 tsp ground coriander

2.5 ml/½ tsp each of ground cumin, ground cinnamon and crushed chilli

600 ml/1 pt/2½ cups vegetable stock

30 ml/2 tbsp tomato purée (paste)

5 ml/1 tsp dried mint

5 ml/1 tsp dried oregano

Salt and ground black pepper

This recipe uses mainly store-cupboard ingredients. Replace the dried herbs with fresh if you have them (use about three times the quantity of fresh compared to dry). It's good served in bowls with hot and crusty garlic bread.

1

Put the chickpeas, kidney beans, tomatoes, barley, carrots and parsnips into the slo-cooker.

2

Heat the oil in a frying pan (skillet) and add the onion, garlic and spices. Cook for a few minutes, stirring occasionally, without browning.

3

Add the remaining ingredients to the frying pan, bring just to the boil and pour over the contents of the slo-cooker, stirring gently. (If you are using fresh herbs, add these for the final 30 minutes cooking only.)

4

Cover and cook on LOW for 8–10 hours.

5

Stir well before serving.

Cooking time
8–10 hours on LOW

Fish

When I first used a slo-cooker, I confess to attempting to cook everything in it. Fish was one of my less successful ventures, for although it retains its shape during slow cooking, it can dry out and toughen if cooked for too long and it is difficult to lift out of the slo-cooker in one piece. These days, I use the slo-cooker to cook fish only very simply for a relatively short time (see Tips for Fish, below), or to cook one or two specific recipes. After all, most fish can be cooked in minutes on the hob or under the grill (broiler), so I would prefer to use the slo-cooker to prepare a vegetable dish or perhaps a pudding – something that can be left to cook all day.

Having said that, I like to add bite-sized pieces of my favourite fish to vegetable soups or casseroles made in the slo-cooker – pop them in for just the last 20 minutes of cooking time. Try adding white fish to Fresh Tomato Soup (see page 26) or smoked haddock to Leek and Potato Soup (see page 30 – you don't even have to bother to purée it).

Basic method for cooking fish

- Grease the inside of the slo-cooker with oil, butter or margarine.
- Arrange whole small fish or fish fillets in a single layer in the slo-cooker (you may need to remove heads and tails to fit them in).
- Dot with butter or margarine and sprinkle with chopped herbs, grated lemon rind and/or chopped spring onions.
- Add 30–45 ml/2–3 tbsp liquid – this may be water, wine, cider, stock or fruit juice.
- Cover and cook on LOW for 3–4 hours or HIGH for 1–2 hours.

Mackerel and monkfish bake

25 g/1 oz/2 tbsp butter or
  margarine

1 onion, finely chopped

100 g/4 oz button mushrooms,
  sliced

225 g/8 oz tomatoes, skinned and
  sliced

Juice of 1 lemon

45 ml/3 tbsp water

Salt and freshly ground black
  pepper

450 g/1 lb mackerel fillets, skinned
  and cut into pieces

450 g/1 lb monkfish fillets,
  skinned and cut into pieces

Finely chopped parsley, to garnish

Vary your choice of fish by replacing the mackerel with salmon or smoked haddock and the monkfish with haddock, plaice or cod. It's delicious served with crisp fried (sautéed) bread or hot toast.

Heat the butter or margarine in a saucepan and cook the onion for about 5 minutes, stirring occasionally, until softened but not browned. Stir in the mushrooms, tomatoes, lemon juice and 45 ml/3 tbsp water and season lightly.

Stir in the mackerel and monkfish and transfer to the slo-cooker.

Cover and cook on LOW for 2–4 hours.

Serve scattered with chopped parsley.

Cooking time
2–4 hours on LOW

Haddock and courgettes in wine

700 g/1½ lb haddock, cod, or other white fish, skinned and cut into pieces

15 ml/1 tbsp cornflour (cornstarch)

15 ml/1 tbsp olive oil

1 onion, finely chopped

1 garlic clove, crushed

225 g/8 oz courgettes (zucchini), thinly sliced

300 ml/½ pt/1¼ cups dry white wine or cider

1 bay leaf

30 ml/2 tbsp finely chopped fresh herbs, such as dill, fennel, tarragon or parsley

I like to serve this with a crisp green salad and new potatoes.

1

Toss the fish in the cornflour until it is well coated, shaking off any excess.

2

Heat the oil in a frying pan (skillet) and cook the onion and garlic for about 5 minutes, stirring occasionally, without browning.

3

Stir in the courgettes, then the wine or cider and the bay leaf. Bring just to the boil, stir in the fish, then transfer to the slo-cooker.

4

Cover and cook on LOW for 3–5 hours.

5

Just before serving, gently stir in the herbs.

Cooking time
3–5 hours on LOW

Rollmop herrings

8 herring fillets, boned

Salt

150 ml/¼ pt/⅔ cup wine vinegar

3 shallots, very thinly sliced

1 gherkin (cornichon), finely
    chopped

2 bay leaves

1 finely pared strip of lemon zest

10 black peppercorns

Ask your fishmonger to prepare the herring fillets for you. Small mackerel fillets are ideal for this recipe too. Serve it warm or cold with crusty bread or new potatoes.

1

Season the herring fillets lightly with salt. Roll up from the tail end, skin-side out, and arrange in the slo-cooker.

2

Put the remaining ingredients in a saucepan with 150 ml/¼ pt/⅔ cup water and a seasoning of salt. Bring to the boil and pour over the herrings.

3

Cover and cook on LOW for 3–5 hours.

4

Arrange the herrings in a serving dish, pour over the cooking liquor and leave to cool.

Cooking time
3–5 hours on LOW

Stuffed plaice in orange sauce

50 g/ 2 oz/¼ cup butter or margarine

100 g/4 oz button or closed-cup mushrooms, chopped

2 hard-boiled (hard-cooked) eggs, finely chopped

2.5 ml/½ tsp finely grated orange rind

Salt and freshly ground black pepper

8 plaice fillets, skinned

Juice of 2 oranges

This is delicious served on a bed of rice cooked with peas and sweetcorn (corn).

1

Heat 15 g/½ oz/1 tbsp of the butter or margarine in a saucepan and cook the mushrooms for about 2 minutes, stirring occasionally. Stir in the eggs and orange rind and season to taste.

2

Spoon a little of the mixture on to the skinned side of each fillet. Roll up and secure with cocktail sticks (toothpicks).

3

Arrange the fish in the slo-cooker, dot with the remaining butter or margarine and add the orange juice.

4

Cover and cook on LOW for 2½–3½ hours.

Cooking time
2½–3½ hours on LOW

Italian fish

25 g/1 oz/2 tbsp butter or margarine

2 tomatoes, skinned and sliced

1 red (bell) pepper, thinly sliced

100 g/4 oz closed-cup mushrooms, sliced

15 ml/1 tbsp finely chopped fresh parsley

Salt and freshly ground black pepper

4 whole fish, such as red mullet or trout, about 175–225 g/6–8 oz each

60 ml/4 tbsp red or white wine

15 ml/1 tbsp snipped fresh chives

Choose fish that will fit easily into the slo-cooker (remove heads and tails if necessary).

Grease the slo-cooker with a little of the butter or margarine. Layer the tomatoes, pepper and mushrooms in the slo-cooker, sprinkling with the parsley and seasoning with salt and pepper.

Season the fish lightly, inside and out and arrange them on top of the vegetables. Pour the wine over and dot with the remaining butter.

Cover and cook on HIGH for 2–3 hours.

Serve sprinkled with the chives.

Cooking time
2–3 hours on HIGH

Skate in tomato and olive sauce

- 25 g/1 oz/2 tbsp butter or margarine, plus extra for greasing
- 4 skate pieces, total weight about 700 g/1½ lb
- Salt and freshly ground black pepper
- 1 onion, finely chopped
- 5 ml/1 tsp sugar
- 200 g/7 oz/1 small can of chopped tomatoes
- 30 ml/2 tbsp tomato purée (paste)
- 8 green pimento-stuffed olives

I love the meatiness of skate, which suits this recipe well. Try it also with other firm white fish, such as monkfish. For a change, try using capers instead of stuffed olives.

1 Grease the inside of the slo-cooker with a little of the butter or margarine. Lightly sprinkle the skate pieces with salt and pepper and arrange them in the slo-cooker.

2 Heat the remaining butter or margarine in a saucepan and cook the onion with the sugar for about 5 minutes, stirring occasionally, without browning.

3 Add the remaining ingredients, season lightly and bring to the boil. Pour gently over the skate in the slo-cooker.

4 Cover and cook on LOW for 2½–3½ hours.

Cooking time
2½–3½ hours on LOW

Meat, Poultry and Game

This is possibly where the slo-cooker gives its best performances. Pot-roasts, casseroles and old-fashioned meat puddings are ideal for its gentle, leisurely tenderising. There's no need for checking, basting, turning and stirring, there's little risk of burning or overcooking, and large pieces of meat show only minimum shrinkage. Best of all, the flavours that develop are just wonderful!

Quick tips for meat, poultry and game

- Use lean meat and trim off excess fat before using.
- Make sure that meat joints and whole birds will fit comfortably in the slo-cooker with the lid comfortably in place. Tying or trussing with cook's string gives you something to grip and enables easy removal of the cooked joint or bird from the slo-cooker.
- For casseroles, cut meat into even, bite-size pieces. (Remember that vegetables can take longer to cook than meat so cut them into small pieces or slice them thinly.)
- Brown meat, poultry or game in a little oil in a saucepan on the hob before adding to the slo-cooker – this adds lots of flavour and colour to the finished dish.
- Cooking liquids can be stock, wine, beer, cider, fruit juice or water.
- Bring the cooking liquor to the boil before pouring over the meat in the slo-cooker. You will need about half the liquid that you would use in a conventional recipe.
- Stir dishes that contain a lot of liquid, such as casseroles, before serving.
- Season lightly with salt and pepper. You can always adjust the seasoning to taste just before serving.
- Dumplings can be added to the top of a stew or casserole for the final 30 minutes of cooking time. Switch the heat setting to HIGH before adding them.

- Pork joints and whole birds should always be cooked on HIGH. Other joints, chicken and game portions and cut meat are all suitable for cooking on LOW or HIGH.
- If using cream to thicken a sauce, add it for the final 30 minutes cooking time only.

- Cooking times will vary according to shape, size and quality of the meat, poultry or game and according to your personal taste. Here is a guide:

Joint of beef, lamb, veal or venison	1.25–1.5 kg/2½–3 lb	LOW 4–10 hours HIGH 3–6 hours
	1.6–2.25 kg/3½–5 lb	LOW 7–12 hours HIGH 5–8 hours
Joint of pork	1.25–1.5 kg/2½–3 lb	HIGH 3–5 hours (Do not cook on LOW)
	1.6–2.25 kg/3½–5 lb	HIGH 4–6 hours (Do not cook on LOW)
Chicken, whole	1.5 kg/3 lb	HIGH 3½–4 hours (Do not cook on LOW)
Duck, whole	1.75 kg/4 lb	HIGH 5–6 hours (Do not cook on LOW)
Pheasant and guinea fowl, whole	Large	HIGH 3–4 hours (Do not cook on LOW)

Hungarian beef

45 ml/3 tbsp plain (all-purpose) flour

Salt and freshly ground black pepper

1 kg/2¼ lb lean stewing steak, cut into cubes

45 ml/3 tbsp oil

2 large onions, thinly sliced

2 red or green (bell) peppers, thinly sliced

1 garlic clove, crushed

300 ml/½ pt/1¼ cups beef stock

400 g/14 oz/1 large can of chopped tomatoes

45 ml/3 tbsp tomato purée (paste)

15 ml/1 tbsp paprika

2.5 ml/½ tsp grated nutmeg

60 ml/4 tbsp soured (dairy-sour) cream or plain yoghurt

Chopped fresh parsley, to garnish

This rich beef stew, traditionally flavoured with paprika, is good served with rice.

Season the flour with salt and pepper, then toss the meat in the flour, shaking off any excess.

Heat the oil in a large frying pan (skillet) and brown the meat lightly on all sides (you may need to do this in batches). Transfer to the slo-cooker.

Add the onions, peppers and garlic to the pan and cook for about 8 minutes stirring occasionally, without browning.

Stir in the stock, tomatoes, tomato purée, paprika and nutmeg and bring just to the boil. Transfer to the slo-cooker.

Cover and cook on LOW for 7–10 hours.

Just before serving, adjust the seasoning to taste, stir in the cream or yoghurt and sprinkle with parsley to garnish.

Cooking time
7–10 hours on LOW

Italian-style beef in wine

45 ml/3 tbsp olive oil

750 g/1¾ lb braising steak, trimmed and cut into cubes

1 large onion, chopped

1 garlic clove, crushed

500 ml/17 fl oz/2¼ cups red wine

15 ml/1 tbsp tomato purée (paste)

5 ml/1 tsp sugar

Salt and freshly ground back pepper

A few sprigs of fresh thyme

200 ml/7 fl oz/scant 1 cup beef stock

20 ml/1½ tbsp cornflour (cornstarch)

100 g/4 oz button mushrooms

425 g/15 oz/1 large can of artichoke hearts, drained and halved

12 black olives, stoned (pitted)

Chopped fresh herbs, to garnish

Tagliatelle, to serve

1
Put 15 ml/1 tbsp of the oil into a non-metallic container and add the steak. Mix together the onion, garlic, wine, tomato purée, sugar, seasoning and thyme and pour over. Stir well, cover and leave to marinate overnight in the fridge.

2
Strain off the marinade and reserve.

3
Heat the remaining oil in a large saucepan and brown the meat and onion mixture in batches, transferring each batch to the slo-cooker.

4
Tip the reserved marinade into the saucepan and add the stock. Bring to the boil and pour over the beef.

5
Cover and cook on LOW for 8–10 hours. About 40 minutes before the end of cooking time, blend the cornflour with a little cold water to make a smooth paste and stir into the slo-cooker with the mushrooms, artichokes and olives.

6
Sprinkle with fresh herbs and serve with tagliatelle tossed in butter.

Cooking time
8–10 hours on LOW

Beef and orange casserole

30 ml/2 tbsp oil

450 g/1 lb lean stewing steak, cut into cubes

2 onions, chopped

1 carrot, cut into small dice

15 ml/1 tbsp plain (all-purpose) flour

300 ml/½ pt/1¼ cups beef stock

175 g/6 oz button mushrooms

400 g/14 oz/1 large can of chopped tomatoes

1 bouquet garni (sachet)

Finely grated rind and juice of 1 orange

Salt and freshly ground black pepper

Try serving this with a green vegetable and mounds of creamy mashed potato, mixed with a dollop of mustard or horseradish sauce.

Heat the oil in a frying pan (skillet) and quickly brown the meat (you may need to do this in batches). Transfer to slo-cooker.

Add the onions and carrot to the pan and cook, stirring occasionally, for 5–10 minutes until soft and just beginning to brown.

Stir in the flour, then gradually stir in the stock. Add the remaining ingredients and bring just to the boil. Pour over the beef in the slo-cooker.

Cover and cook on LOW for 7–9 hours.

Remove the bouquet garni and adjust seasoning to taste before serving.

Cooking time
7–9 hours on LOW

Sweet and sour beef

425 g/15 oz/1 large can of
   pineapple chunks in syrup

30 ml/2 tbsp oil

700 g/1½ lb lean stewing steak, cut
   into cubes

1 onion, chopped

2 celery sticks, thinly sliced

30 ml/2 tbsp cornflour (cornstarch)

300 ml/½ pt/1¼ cups beef stock

30 ml/2 tbsp soy sauce

30 ml/2 tbsp tomato ketchup

45 ml/3 tbsp wine vinegar

Salt and freshly ground black
   pepper

This is delicious served on a bed of rice.

1

Drain the pineapple and reserve. Make the juice up to 450 ml/¾ pt/2 cups with water.

2

Heat the oil in a frying pan (skillet) and quickly brown the meat (you may need to do this in batches). Transfer to the slo-cooker.

3

Add the onion and celery to the pan and cook for about 5 minutes, stirring occasionally, until just beginning to turn golden brown.

4

Stir in the cornflour, then gradually stir in the stock and the reserved pineapple juice. Add all the remaining ingredients, except the pineapple. Bring just to the boil and pour over the beef in the slo-cooker.

5

Cover and cook on LOW for 8–10 hours.

6

Stir in the reserved pineapple for the final 30 minutes to 1 hour.

Cooking time
8–10 hours on LOW

Beef stroganoff

50 g/2 oz/¼ cup butter or margarine

2 onions, finely chopped

30 ml/2 tbsp plain (all-purpose) flour

Salt and freshly ground black pepper

700 g/1¼ lb lean braising steak, cut into thin slices

300 ml/½ pt/1¼ cups beef stock

100 g/4 oz mushrooms, thickly sliced

5 ml/1 tsp dried mixed herbs

15 ml/1 tbsp tomato purée (paste)

15 ml/1 tbsp wholegrain mustard

150 ml/¼ pt/⅔ cup soured (dairy-sour) cream

15 ml/1 tbsp chopped fresh parsley

This recipe is based on the dish that is named after a nineteenth-century Russian diplomat. Serve it with rice.

1

Heat the butter or margarine in a large saucepan and cook the onions for about 5 minutes, stirring occasionally, without browning.

2

Season the flour with salt and pepper, then toss the meat in the flour, shaking off any excess.

3

Add the meat to the onions and cook, stirring occasionally, until browned.

4

Stir in the stock, mushrooms, herbs, tomato purée and mustard. Bring just to the boil, then transfer to the slo-cooker.

5

Cover and cook on LOW for 7–10 hours.

6

Just before serving, stir well, swirl the cream on top and garnish with the parsley.

Cooking time
7–10 hours on LOW

Beef bourguignon

15 ml/1 tbsp oil

25 g/1 oz/2 tbsp butter or
margarine

225 g/8 oz lean streaky bacon,
rinded and finely chopped

2 garlic cloves, crushed

1 kg/2¼ lb lean stewing steak, cut
into cubes

30 ml/2 tbsp plain (all-purpose)
flour

300 ml/½ pt/1¼ cups red wine,
preferably Burgundy

10 ml/2 tsp dried mixed herbs

18 whole baby (pearl) onions or
shallots

Salt and freshly ground black
pepper

*Serve this French classic with new potatoes and a green
vegetable.*

1

Heat the oil and butter or margarine in a large
frying pan (skillet) and cook the bacon and garlic
for about 5 minutes, stirring occasionally.

2

Add the steak and cook, stirring occasionally,
until lightly browned on all sides.

3

Stir in the flour, then gradually stir in the red
wine. Add the herbs, onions and seasoning. Bring
just to the boil, then transfer to the slo-cooker.

4

Cover and cook on LOW for 7–10 hours.

5

Adjust the seasoning to taste before serving.

Cooking time
7–10 hours on LOW

Beef with herb dumplings

1.5 kg/3 lb lean beef joint, such as brisket or silverside

Salt and freshly ground black pepper

15 ml/1 tbsp oil

2 onions, sliced

4 carrots, sliced

1 parsnip, cut into cubes

12 baby potatoes

30 ml/2 tbsp wholegrain mustard

For the dumplings:

100 g/4 oz/1 cup self-raising (self-rising) flour

5 ml/1 tsp baking powder (baking soda)

50 g/2 oz/generous ½ cup shredded (chopped) suet

Salt and freshly ground black pepper

30 ml/2 tbsp chopped fresh mixed herbs, such as parsley, thyme, sage, oregano

Make sure to buy a joint of beef that fits neatly into your slo-cooker, leaving room on top for the dumplings.

1

Season the beef joint lightly all over with salt and pepper.

2

Heat the oil in a large non-stick frying pan (skillet) and brown the beef quickly on all sides. Transfer to the slo-cooker.

3

Add the vegetables to the frying pan and cook for 5–10 minutes, stirring occasionally until golden brown. Scatter them around the beef in the slo-cooker.

4

Add about 600 ml/1 pt/2½ cups water to the frying pan, scraping up any sediments, and stir in the mustard. Bring to the boil and pour just enough into the slo-cooker to cover the vegetables. Cover and cook on LOW for 8–10 hours.

5

To make the dumplings, sift the flour with the baking powder and stir in the suet, seasonings and herbs. Mix in sufficient cold water to make a firm dough. Divide the mixture into eight balls and arrange in the liquid around the beef.

6

Cover and cook for a further 30–40 minutes on HIGH.

Cooking time
8–10 hours on LOW, 30–40 minutes on HIGH

Bolognese sauce

15 ml/1 tbsp oil

1 large onion, finely chopped

2 carrots, finely chopped

1 celery stick, finely chopped

2 lean streaky bacon rashers
(slices), rinded and finely
chopped

2 garlic cloves, crushed

500 g/18 oz minced (ground) beef

150 ml/¼ pt/⅔ cup beef stock

30 ml/2 tbsp tomato purée (paste)

5 ml/1 tsp dried oregano

Salt and freshly ground black
pepper

Serve this in bowls with garlic bread, or tossed with freshly cooked spaghetti or piled into split jacket potatoes. It can also be adapted to make Chilli con Carne – just add a 425 g/15 oz/large can of red kidney beans, drained, at step 3 and stir in chilli powder to taste.

1

Heat the oil in a large saucepan and add the onion, carrots, celery, bacon and garlic. Cook for about 8 minutes, stirring occasionally, without browning.

2

Crumble in the beef and cook, stirring occasionally, until browned and well broken up.

3

Stir in the stock, tomato purée and oregano and season with salt and pepper. Bring just to the boil, then transfer to the slo-cooker.

4

Cover and cook on LOW for 5–8 hours.

Cooking time
5–8 hours on LOW

Above **Hungarian Beef**
(page 65)

Left **Tagliatelle with Bolognese Sauce**
(page 72)

Right **Sweet and Sour Sauce**
(page 39)

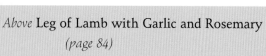

Above Leg of Lamb with Garlic and Rosemary
(page 84)

Above right Oxtail Casserole with Redcurrant Jelly
(page 76)

Right Beef in Brown Ale
(page 74)

Steak and ale pudding

175 g/6 oz/1½ cups self-raising (self-rising) flour

A pinch of salt

75 g/3 oz/¾ cup shredded (chopped) suet

700 g/1½ lb lean stewing steak, cut into cubes

1 onion, finely chopped

30 ml/2 tbsp chopped fresh herbs, such as parsley, thyme or sage

15 ml/1 tbsp plain (all-purpose) flour

Salt and freshly ground black pepper

Beef stock or water

This is the basis for Steak and Kidney Pudding too – just replace 225 g/8 oz of the steak with the same amount of chopped kidneys.

1

Sift the flour and salt into a large bowl and add the suet. Stir in sufficient cold water to make a firm dough. Cut off one quarter, roll into a ball and reserve. On a lightly floured surface, roll out the remaining dough.

2

Lightly butter a 1.2 litre/2 pt/5 cup pudding basin, then line it with the large piece of dough, pressing the edges together and allowing the pastry (paste) to overlap the top of the basin slightly.

3

Combine the steak, onion, herbs, flour and seasonings and spoon the mixture into the lined basin. Add sufficient beef stock or water to come about three-quarters of the way up the filling.

4

On a lightly floured surface, roll out the reserved pastry into a circle, slightly larger than the top of the basin. Lay it on the top and seal well by pressing the pastry edges together.

5

Cover securely with buttered foil and stand the basin in the slo-cooker. Pour round sufficient water to come halfway up the sides of the basin. Cover and cook on HIGH for 6–8 hours.

Cooking time
6–8 hours on HIGH

Beef in brown ale

30 ml/2 tbsp olive oil

4 bacon rashers (slices), rinded and chopped

450 g/1 lb whole baby (pearl) onions

45 ml/3 tbsp plain (all-purpose) flour

Salt and freshly ground black pepper

1 kg/2¼ lb lean stewing steak, cut into pieces

450 ml/¾ pt/2 cups brown ale

15 ml/1 tbsp Dijon mustard

15 ml/ 1 tbsp sugar

5 ml/1 tsp dried mixed herbs

To serve, top this rich casserole with French bread slices that have been toasted and spread with mustard. Arrange them on the casserole, mustard-side down.

1

Heat 15 ml/1 tbsp of the oil in a large saucepan and cook the bacon, stirring occasionally, until crisp and golden brown. With a slotted spoon transfer to the slo-cooker.

2

Add the onions to the saucepan and cook quickly, stirring, until lightly browned. Transfer to the slo-cooker.

3

Season the flour with salt and pepper and toss the steak in it, coating it well.

4

Add the remaining oil to the saucepan and brown the meat quickly on all sides – you may need to do this in batches, transferring each batch to the slo-cooker.

5

Add the ale to the saucepan with the mustard, sugar and herbs. Bring to the boil and pour into the slo-cooker, stirring gently.

6

Cover and cook on LOW for 7–9 hours. Stir before serving.

Cooking time
7–9 hours on LOW

Spicy sausage, bean and potato

30 ml/2 tbsp oil

1 onion, finely chopped

450 g/1 lb small potatoes, thinly sliced

450 g/1 lb small sausages, skinned if preferred

425 g/15 oz/1 large can of baked beans in tomato sauce

100 g/4 oz button mushrooms, halved

150 ml/¼ pt/⅔ cup vegetable stock

5 ml/1 tsp chilli sauce

15 ml/1 tbsp tomato purée (paste)

Salt and freshly ground black pepper

This is usually a favourite with youngsters. Serve it with plenty of hot garlic bread.

1

Heat the oil in a large saucepan and cook the onion and potatoes for about 5 minutes, stirring occasionally.

2

Stir in the remaining ingredients and bring just to the boil. Transfer to the slo-cooker.

3

Cover and cook on LOW for 6–10 hours.

Cooking time
6–10 hours on LOW

Oxtail casserole with redcurrant jelly

15 ml/1 tbsp oil

100 g/4 oz lean streaky bacon, rinded and chopped

1 large onion, thinly sliced

2 carrots, thinly sliced

1 kg/2¼ lb oxtail pieces

A little flour

Salt and freshly ground black pepper

600 ml/1 pt/2½ cups beef stock or half stock and half red wine

30 ml/2 tbsp tomato purée (paste)

5 ml/1 tsp dried mixed herbs

30 ml/2 tbsp redcurrant jelly (optional)

The slo-cooker is ideal for cooking oxtail until it falls off the bone. The redcurrant jelly (clear conserve) is optional – but delicious!

1

Heat the oil in a large saucepan and add the bacon, onion and carrots. Cook for 5–10 minutes, stirring occasionally, until beginning to turn golden brown. Using a slotted spoon, transfer to the slo-cooker.

2

Toss the oxtail pieces in the flour, seasoned with a little salt and pepper to taste, shaking off the excess. Add them to the hot saucepan and brown quickly on all sides. Transfer to the slo-cooker.

3

Stir the stock, tomato purée and herbs into the saucepan. Bring to the boil and pour over the contents of the slo-cooker.

4

Cover and cook on LOW for 8–12 hours.

5

When ready to serve, use a slotted spoon to lift the meat and vegetables on to a serving plate. Keep warm.

6

Allow the juices in the slo-cooker to settle so that the fat rises to the top. Either skim off the fat with a spoon or mop it up with kitchen paper (paper towels). Add the redcurrant jelly into the remaining juices and stir until dissolved.

7

Adjust the seasoning to taste and serve with the meat and vegetables.

Cooking time
8–12 hours on LOW

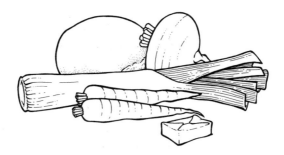

Kleftiko

4 lamb shanks, about 225–350 g/
8–12 oz each

2–3 garlic cloves, cut into slivers

15 ml/1 tbsp olive oil

2 carrots, thinly sliced

8–12 whole baby (pearl) onions

2 celery sticks, thinly sliced

8 baby potatoes, halved

200 g/7 oz/1 small can of chopped
tomatoes

30 ml/2 tbsp lemon juice

Salt and freshly ground black
pepper

15 ml/1 tbsp dried oregano

15 ml/1 tbsp dried mint

This traditional Greek dish, flavoured with oregano and mint, is often prepared in individual foil parcels and baked in the oven. I like to cook it in my slo-cooker, using lamb shanks.

With a sharp knife, make several small incisions in each lamb shank. Insert a sliver of garlic into each one.

Heat the oil in a large saucepan and brown the lamb quickly on all sides. Lift out and set aside.

Add the vegetables to the saucepan and cook for about 5 minutes, stirring occasionally, without browning. Add the tomatoes and bring just to the boil. Pour into the slo-cooker, scraping up any sediment from the bottom of the saucepan.

Lay the lamb shanks on top of the vegetables, pushing them down gently. Sprinkle with lemon juice, salt, pepper, oregano and mint.

Cover and cook on LOW for 10–12 hours until the lamb pulls easily away from the bone. If convenient, turn the lamb and spoon the juices over it once or twice during the final half of cooking time.

6

With a slotted spoon, lift the lamb on to a serving plate and keep warm. Leave to stand, while the juices settle a little and any fat rises to the surface.

7

Spoon off the fat, or mop up with kitchen paper (paper towels).

8

Serve with the sauce and vegetables spooned over the lamb.

Cooking time
10–12 hours on LOW

Lamb with garlic, rosemary and ginger serves 4

4 lamb shanks, about 225–350 g/
  8–12 oz each

1 onion, thinly sliced

2 garlic cloves, thinly sliced

2.5 cm/1 in piece of fresh root
  ginger, thinly sliced

10 black peppercorns

350 ml/12 fl oz/1⅓ cups red wine

2 sprigs of fresh rosemary

Salt and freshly ground black
  pepper

30 ml/2 tbsp olive oil

300 ml/½ pt/1¼ cups lamb stock

400 g/14 oz/1 large can of chopped
  tomatoes

30 ml/2 tbsp tomato purée (paste)

10 ml/2 tsp sugar

Put the lamb shanks, in a single layer, in a shallow, non-metallic dish. Spoon over the onion, garlic, ginger, peppercorns, wine and rosemary. Cover and marinate in the fridge overnight, turning the lamb occasionally, if possible.

Tip the contents of the dish into a large sieve (strainer) over a bowl. Lift out the lamb, pat dry with kitchen paper (paper towels) and season lightly all over with salt and pepper.

Heat the oil in a large saucepan and quickly brown the lamb on all sides. With a slotted spoon, transfer them to the slo-cooker.

Add the onion mixture from the sieve to the saucepan and cook for about 5 minutes, stirring occasionally, until just beginning to turn golden brown. Add the reserved marinade and the stock, tomatoes, tomato purée and sugar. Bring to the boil and pour over the lamb in the slo-cooker.

Cover and cook on LOW for 10–12 hours until the lamb pulls easily away from the bone. Using a slotted spoon, lift the lamb on to a serving plate and keep warm. Leave to stand while the juices settle a little and any fat rises to the surface. Remove and discard the fat. Serve the sauce and vegetables spooned over the lamb.

Cooking time
10–12 hours on LOW

Lamb with gremolada

60 ml/4 tbsp plain (all-purpose) flour

Salt and freshly ground black pepper

4 lamb leg steaks, 175 g/6 oz each

30 ml/2 tbsp olive oil

1 onion, finely chopped

2 carrots, finely chopped

1 garlic clove, finely chopped

60 ml/4 tbsp dry white wine

400 g/14 oz/1 large can of chopped tomatoes

200 ml/7 fl oz/scant 1 cup lamb or chicken stock

30 ml/2 tbsp tomato purée (paste)

5 ml/1 tsp dried rosemary

For the gremolada:

Finely grated rind of 1 lemon

45 ml/3 tbsp finely chopped fresh parsley

1–2 garlic cloves, crushed

Gremolada is a garnish made of finely chopped parsley, grated lemon rind and crushed garlic. It adds a really fresh flavour to the richness of the lamb and sauce.

Put the flour into a freezer bag and season with salt and pepper. Add one lamb steak, close the bag and shake until coated. Lift out, shaking off excess flour. Repeat with the remaining lamb steaks.

Heat the oil in a large frying pan (skillet) and quickly brown the lamb on both sides. Lift out.

Add the onion, carrots and garlic to the pan and cook for about 5 minutes, stirring occasionally, until only just beginning to brown. Stir in any flour remaining in the bag.

Gradually stir in the wine, then add the tomatoes, stock, tomato purée and rosemary. Season with salt and pepper. Bring just to the boil and pour into the slo-cooker. Lay the lamb steaks on top. Cover and cook on LOW for 6–8 hours.

Just before serving, mix together the gremolada ingredients. Serve the lamb, vegetables and sauce topped with the gremolada.

Cooking time
6–8 hours on LOW

Lamb in mushroom sauce

15 ml/1 tbsp olive oil

15 g/½ oz/1 tbsp butter or margarine

2 onions, thinly sliced

1 garlic clove, crushed

1 red (bell) pepper, thinly sliced

750 g/1¾ lb lean lamb shoulder, cubed

100 g/4 oz mushrooms, sliced

295 g/11 oz/1 medium can of condensed mushroom soup

5 ml/1 tsp dried mixed herbs

Salt and freshly ground black pepper

In this quick and simple dish, a can of good-quality soup provides a speedy, flavoursome base for the sauce.

1

Heat the oil and butter or margarine in a large frying pan (skillet) and cook the onions, garlic and pepper for about 5 minutes, stirring occasionally, without browning.

2

Add the lamb and cook quickly until browned on all sides.

3

Stir in the mushrooms, soup, herbs and seasonings. Bring just to the boil, then transfer to the slo-cooker.

4

Cover and cook on LOW for 6–8 hours.

Cooking time
6–8 hours on LOW

Lamb and onions in a red wine sauce

15 ml/1 tbsp olive oil

2 red onions, thinly sliced

5 ml/1 tsp sugar

8 lean lamb chops

Salt and freshly ground black
    pepper

15 ml/1 tbsp cornflour (cornstarch)

300 ml/½ pt/1¼ cups red wine

10 ml/2 tsp dried rosemary

1

Heat the oil in a frying pan (skillet)) and cook the onions with the sugar for about 10 minutes, stirring occasionally, until golden brown. Transfer to the slo-cooker.

2

Season the lamb with salt and pepper then, in the same pan, brown on all sides.

3

Arrange the chops on top of the onions in the slo-cooker.

4

Stir the cornflour into the remaining fat in the pan, then gradually stir in the red wine. Add the rosemary. Bring just to the boil, then pour over the lamb and onions.

5

Cover and cook on LOW for 4–6 hours.

Cooking time
4–6 hours on LOW

Leg of lamb with garlic and rosemary SERVES 6

1.6 kg/3½ lb leg of lamb

2 garlic cloves, thinly sliced

A few sprigs of fresh rosemary

Salt and freshly ground black
 pepper

15 ml/1 tbsp olive oil

15 ml/1 tbsp cornflour (cornstarch)

300 ml/½ pt/1¼ cups dry cider

60 ml/4 tbsp clear honey

Use this recipe as a guide. The size of the lamb joint will depend on the capacity of your slo-cooker.

1

Using a sharp knife, make several small incisions in the lamb. Insert a sliver of garlic and some rosemary leaves into each one. Season the lamb lightly all over with salt and pepper.

2

Heat the oil in a large frying pan (skillet) and brown the lamb quickly on all sides. Transfer to the slo-cooker.

3

Stir the cornflour into the pan, then gradually stir in the cider and honey. Bring just to the boil, stirring continuously. Pour over the lamb, making sure it is well coated.

4

Cook on LOW for 5–10 hours, basting once or twice during last couple of hours if possible.

5

Lift the lamb on to a carving dish and serve the sauce separately.

Cooking time
5–10 hours on LOW

Minted lamb in tomato sauce

15 ml/1 tbsp olive oil

4 lean lamb leg steaks

1 onion, thinly sliced

5 ml/1 tsp sugar

1 garlic clove, crushed

400 g/14 oz/1 large can of chopped
    tomatoes

150 ml/¼ pt/⅔ cup lamb or chicken
    stock

15 ml/1 tbsp chopped fresh mint

Salt and freshly ground black
    pepper

Potato or root vegetable mash goes well with this rich dish.

Heat the oil in a non-stick frying pan (skillet) and brown the lamb steaks quickly on both sides. Transfer to the slo-cooker.

Add the onion and sugar to the pan and cook, stirring occasionally, without browning.

Stir the remaining ingredients into the onions, scraping up any sediment from the bottom of the pan. Bring to the boil and pour over the lamb in the slo-cooker, coating it completely.

Cover and cook on LOW for 4–6 hours.

Cooking time
4–6 hours on LOW

Liver and bacon casserole

30 ml/2 tbsp plain (all-purpose) flour

Salt and freshly ground black pepper

450 g/1 lb liver, cut into 1 cm/ ½ in slices

30 ml/2 tbsp oil

8 back bacon rashers (slices), rinded and chopped

1 onion, thinly sliced

150 ml/¼ pt/⅔ cup beef stock

15 ml/1 tbsp tomato purée (paste)

15 ml/1 tbsp wholegrain mustard

This traditional dish is perfect served with potato or root vegetable mash. Lambs' liver has a wonderful delicate flavour, but pigs' or ox liver will do just as well.

Season the flour with salt and pepper, then toss the liver in the flour, shaking off any excess.

Heat the oil in a frying pan (skillet) and cook the bacon rashers and onion for about 5 minutes until beginning to turn golden brown. With a slotted spoon, transfer the bacon and onion to the slo-cooker.

Add the liver to the pan and cook quickly until golden brown on all sides. Transfer to the slo-cooker.

Stir the stock into the pan with the tomato purée and mustard and bring just to the boil. Season with salt and pepper, then pour into the slo-cooker.

Cover and cook on LOW for 6–8 hours.

Cooking time
6–8 hours on LOW

900 g/2 lb lean best-end-of-neck lamb chops

Salt and freshly ground black pepper

15 ml/1 tbsp olive oil

2 large carrots, thinly sliced

1 large onion, thinly sliced

350 g/12 oz potatoes, cut into 1 cm/½ in cubes

25 ml/1½ tbsp plain (all-purpose) flour

450 ml/¾ pt/2 cups beef stock

10 ml/2 tsp sugar

45 ml/3 tbsp tomato purée (paste)

10 ml/2 tsp dried mixed herbs

This classic French lamb stew is made with onions and potatoes. Serve it with crusty bread.

1

Season the lamb chops with salt and pepper. Heat the oil in a frying pan (skillet) and brown the chops quickly on both sides. Transfer to the slo-cooker.

2

Add the vegetables to the pan and cook for about 5 minutes, stirring occasionally, until beginning to turn golden brown.

3

Stir in the flour, then gradually stir in the stock and all the remaining ingredients. Bring just to the boil, stirring continuously. Transfer to the slo-cooker and stir well.

4

Cover and cook on LOW for 7–10 hours.

5

Adjust the seasoning to taste before serving.

Cooking time
7–10 hours on LOW

Sweet and sour pork chops

15 ml/1 tbsp plain (all-purpose)
flour

Salt and freshly ground black
pepper

4 lean pork chops, trimmed of
excess fat

30 ml/2 tbsp oil

2 onions, finely chopped

90 ml/6 tbsp vegetable stock

60 ml/4 tbsp soy sauce

60 ml/4 tbsp tomato purée (paste)

60 ml/4 tbsp soft brown sugar

60 ml/4 tbsp dry sherry

Plain rice, to serve

Season the flour with salt and pepper, then dust the chops with the flour, shaking off any excess.

Heat the oil in a frying pan (skillet) and brown the chops quickly on all sides. Transfer to the slo-cooker.

Add the onions to the pan and cook for about 5 minutes, stirring occasionally, until beginning to turn golden brown. Stir in the remaining ingredients and bring just to the boil. Pour over the chops in the slo-cooker.

❹

Cover and cook on LOW for 5–8 hours.

Cooking time
5–8 hours on LOW

Pork in apple and cider sauce

15 ml/1 tbsp oil

15 g/½ oz/1 tbsp butter or margarine

1 onion, thinly sliced

2 celery sticks, thinly sliced

1 large cooking (tart) apple, peeled, cored and chopped

750 g/1¾ lb lean pork, cut into cubes

30 ml/2 tbsp plain (all-purpose) flour

300 ml/½ pt/1¼ cups dry or medium cider

Salt and freshly ground black pepper

5 ml/1 tsp dried sage

I like to serve this with tagliatelle and a green salad with some slices of crisp eating (dessert) apple added to it.

1

Heat the oil and butter or margarine in a large saucepan and cook the onion and celery for about 5 minutes, stirring occasionally, without browning. Add the apple and transfer to the slo-cooker.

2

Add the pork to the saucepan and cook quickly until lightly browned on all sides.

3

Stir in the flour, then gradually stir in the cider. Season lightly and add the sage. Bring just to the boil, stirring continuously, then transfer to the slo-cooker and stir well.

4

Cover and cook on LOW for 6–10 hours.

Cooking time
6–10 hours on LOW

Pork and mushroom casserole SERVES 4

15 ml/1 tbsp olive oil

700 g/1½ lb lean pork, cut into cubes

1 large red onion, thinly sliced

30 ml/2 tbsp plain (all-purpose) flour

300 ml/½ pt/1¼ cups white wine

150 ml/¼ pt/⅔ cup chicken stock

30 ml/2 tbsp tomato purée (paste)

1 red or yellow (bell) pepper, sliced

225 g/8 oz closed-cup mushrooms, thickly sliced

5 ml/1 tsp dried sage

Salt and freshly ground black pepper

2 large ripe tomatoes, skinned, seeded and chopped

Freshly cooked rice or pasta makes a good accompaniment to this dish. The tomatoes are stirred in at the last minute – to give a really fresh taste.

1

Heat the oil in a large non-stick frying pan (skillet) and cook the pork quickly until lightly browned – you may need to do this in batches, transferring each batch to the slo-cooker.

2

Add the onion to the pan and cook for a few minutes, stirring occasionally, without browning.

3

Stir in the flour, then gradually stir in the wine and stock. Add the remaining ingredients, except for the tomatoes, and bring to the boil. Pour over the pork in the slo-cooker, stirring gently.

4

Cover and cook on LOW for 6–8 hours.

5

About 30 minutes before serving, adjust the seasoning to taste and stir in the tomatoes.

Cooking time
6–8 hours on LOW

Curried pork with pineapple

30 ml/2 tbsp plain (all-purpose) flour

Salt and freshly ground black pepper

1 kg/2¼ lb lean pork, cut into cubes

30 ml/2 tbsp oil

1 large onion, finely chopped

30 ml/2 tbsp curry paste

15 ml/1 tbsp paprika

300 ml/½ pt/1¼ cups chicken stock

30 ml/2 tbsp mango chutney, chopped

5 ml/1 tsp Worcestershire sauce

425 g/15 oz/1 large can of pineapple cubes in syrup

Plain rice, to serve

Serve this with rice and poppadoms.

1

Season the flour with salt and pepper, then toss the pork pieces in the mixture until coated.

2

Heat the oil in a frying pan (skillet) and brown the meat quickly on all sides. Transfer to the slo-cooker.

3

Add the onion to the pan and cook for about 5 minutes, stirring occasionally, without browning. Add the remaining ingredients and bring just to the boil. Transfer to the slo-cooker and stir well.

4

Cover and cook on LOW for 5–8 hours.

Cooking time
5–8 hours on LOW

Glazed bacon with red onions SERVES 6–8

1 lean bacon joint, such as prime
   collar or gammon, about
   1.25 kg/2½ lb

2 red onions, thinly sliced

15 ml/1 tbsp fresh thyme leaves

Freshly ground black pepper

300 ml/½ pt/1¼ cups hot chicken
   stock

For the glaze:

30 ml/2 tbsp brown sugar

30 ml/2 tbsp wholegrain mustard

Make sure to choose a bacon joint that will fit your slo-cooker. Use this recipe as a basis for cooking lean lamb and beef joints too.

①

Put the bacon in a large saucepan, cover with cold water and bring slowly to the boil. Drain and discard the water.

②

Arrange the onions in the base of the slo-cooker and sprinkle the thyme leaves over. Season with black pepper.

③

Sit the bacon on the bed of onions and pour the hot stock over. Cover and cook on LOW for 7–9 hours until cooked through.

④

To glaze the bacon, carefully lift it out of the slo-cooker and cut off the rind, leaving a thin layer of fat. Score the fat with a sharp knife in a criss-cross pattern. Combine the sugar and mustard and, with a flat knife or the back of a spoon, spread the mixture over the fatty surface. Put under a hot grill (broiler) until bubbling and golden.

⑤

With a slotted spoon, lift the onions out of the slo-cooker and keep warm. Spoon any excess fat from the surface of the juices or soak it up with kitchen paper (paper towels). Adjust the seasoning and spoon the juice over the onions. Serve with the bacon.

Cooking time
7–9 hours on LOW

Malay spiced pork

30 ml/2 tbsp curry paste

30 ml/2 tbsp tomato purée (paste)

30 ml/2 tbsp mango chutney, chopped if necessary

Finely grated rind and juice of 1 lemon

50 g/2 oz/⅓ cup sultanas (golden raisins)

250 g/9 oz/1 carton plain yoghurt

900 g/2 lb lean pork, such as shoulder, cut into cubes

15 ml/1 tbsp oil

1 large onion, thinly sliced

30 ml/2 tbsp plain (all-purpose) flour

300 ml/½ pt/1¼ cups chicken stock

45 ml/3 tbsp finely chopped creamed coconut

2 large eating (dessert) apples, peeled, cored and chopped

Salt and freshly ground black pepper

Best results are obtained if the pork is marinated in the spicy mixture for a few hours or overnight. Plain rice makes the perfect accompaniment here. I like to serve some crisp poppadoms with it too.

1

Combine the curry paste, tomato purée, mango chutney, lemon rind and juice, sultanas and yoghurt in a large, non-metallic dish. Stir in the pork until well coated, cover and leave to marinate in the fridge for a few hours or overnight. Stir the mixture occasionally if possible.

2

Heat the oil in a large saucepan, add the onion and cook for a few minutes, stirring occasionally, without browning.

3

Stir the flour into the onions, then gradually stir in the chicken stock. Add the pork mixture and the remaining ingredients, bring just to the boil and transfer to the slo-cooker.

4

Cover and cook on LOW for 6–8 hours.

Cooking time
6–8 hours on LOW

Somerset bacon hot-pot

15 ml/1 tbsp olive oil

1 large onion, chopped

2 celery sticks, sliced

3 carrots, sliced

2 parsnips, sliced

30 ml/2 tbsp plain (all-purpose) flour

300 ml/½ pt/1¼ cups apple juice

150 ml/¼ pt/⅔ cup vegetable stock

700 g/1½ lb lean unsmoked bacon, cut into cubes

225 g/8 oz baby salad potatoes, thickly sliced

This recipe was first created using a single variety apple juice from a farm near my home. Use a sharp-tasting variety if you can – it will add an individual flavour. It's delicious served with a mound of fluffy couscous to mop up the juices.

1

Heat the oil in a large saucepan and add the onion, celery, carrots and parsnips. Cook for about 5 minutes, stirring occasionally, without browning.

2

Stir in the flour, then gradually stir in the apple juice and vegetable stock.

3

Put the potatoes into the slo-cooker, followed by the bacon. Pour the vegetable mixture over the top and stir gently.

4

Cover and cook on LOW for 6–8 hours.

Cooking time
6–8 hours on LOW

Pot-roast bacon with apple

*1 unsmoked lean bacon joint, such
   as collar, about 1.75 kg/4 lb,
   skin removed*

Freshly ground black pepper

15 ml/1 tbsp oil

1 large onion, chopped

*2 eating (dessert) apples, peeled,
   cored and thickly sliced*

15 ml/1 tbsp chopped fresh sage

10 ml/2 tsp cornflour (cornstarch)

Put the bacon in a large saucepan, cover with cold water and bring slowly to the boil. Drain and discard the water. Pat the bacon dry with kitchen paper (paper towels) and season all over with freshly ground black pepper.

②

Heat the oil in a large non-stick frying pan (skillet) and quickly brown the bacon on all sides. Transfer to the slo-cooker.

③

Add the onion to the pan and cook for about 5 minutes, stirring occasionally, without browning. Stir in the apples, sage and 150 ml/¼ pt/⅔ cup water. Bring to the boil and pour around the bacon in the slo-cooker. Cover and cook on LOW for 8–10 hours. Lift the bacon on to a warmed serving plate.

④

Spoon off any excess fat from the top of the juices or soak it up with kitchen paper. To thicken the juices, transfer the contents of the slo-cooker to a saucepan. Blend the cornflour with a little cold water to make a smooth paste and stir into the saucepan. Bring to the boil, stirring gently, and simmer gently for 1–2 minutes.

Serve the sauce with the bacon.

Cooking time
8–10 hours on LOW

Cassoulet

SERVES 8

96

225 g/8 oz lean streaky bacon, rinded and cut into pieces

30 ml/2 tbsp olive oil

2 onions, sliced

4 celery sticks, sliced

2 garlic cloves, crushed or finely chopped

450 ml/¾ pt/2 cups chicken stock

2–3 tbsp black treacle (molasses)

30–45 ml/2–3 tbsp wholegrain mustard

Salt and freshly ground black pepper

8 chicken thighs, skinned

225 g/8 oz smoked pork sausage, thickly sliced

2 × 425 g/15 oz/large cans of haricot (navy) beans, drained

Cassoulet is one of my favourite dishes. It's great for feeding crowds, everyone loves it and leftovers freeze well. If you decide to halve the recipe, cook it for 6–8 hours. Serve it with plenty of hot, crusty, garlic bread and a crisp green salad.

Heat the bacon in a non-stick frying pan (skillet) until the fat begins to run out, then cook for a few minutes, stirring occasionally, until browned. Using a slotted spoon, transfer to the slo-cooker.

Add the oil to the pan and stir in the onions, celery and garlic. Cook for about 5 minutes, stirring occasionally, until just beginning to brown. Stir in the stock, treacle, mustard and seasoning. Bring just to the boil, then stir the mixture into the bacon in the slo-cooker.

Arrange the chicken thighs on top, pushing them into the liquid. Add the sausage and the beans, pressing them down gently into the liquid.

Cover and cook on AUTO for 8–10 hours.

Stir gently before serving.

Cooking time
8–10 hours on AUTO

Above Pot-roast Bacon Pot with Apple
(*page 95*)

Above right Pork and Mushroom Casserole
(*page 90*)

Right Curried Pork with Pineapple
(*page 91*)

Above left Pheasant in Cider
(page 112)

Left Spicy Gingered Chicken with Pineapple
(page 98)

Above Steak and Ale Pudding
(page 73)

Bacon and apple pudding

175 g/6 oz/1½ cups self-raising
(self-rising) flour

A pinch of salt

75 g/3 oz/¾ cup shredded
(chopped) suet

10 ml/2 tsp chopped fresh mint

700 g/1½ lb unsmoked bacon joint,
cut into cubes

4 spring onions (scallions), sliced

1 eating (dessert) apple, peeled,
cored and chopped

30 ml/2 tbsp chopped fresh parsley

Freshly ground black pepper

Butter or margarine, for greasing

*The suet pastry in this old fashioned pudding is flavoured
with mint.*

1

Sift the flour and salt into a large bowl and add
the suet and mint. Stir in sufficient cold water to
make a firm dough. Cut off one quarter, roll into a
ball and reserve.

2

Lightly butter a 1.2 litre/2 pt/5 cup pudding
basin.

3

On a lightly floured surface, roll out the large
piece of dough and use it to line the basin, pressing
the edges together well and allowing the pastry to
overlap the top of the basin slightly.

4

Combine the remaining ingredients and spoon
them into the lined basin. Add 45 ml/3 tbsp water.

5

On a lightly floured surface, roll out the
reserved pastry into a circle, and seal it on top of
the pudding.

6

Cover securely with greased foil and stand the
basin in the slo-cooker. Pour round sufficient water
to come halfway up the sides of the basin.

7

Cover and cook on HIGH for 6–8 hours.

Cooking time
6–8 hours on HIGH

Spicy gingered chicken with pineapple SERVES 4

15 ml/1 tbsp oil

4 chicken portions

1 onion, finely chopped

2 celery sticks, chopped

30 ml/2 tbsp plain (all-purpose) flour

150 ml/¼ pt/⅔ cup chicken stock

425 g/15 oz/1 large can of pineapple pieces in fruit juice

10 ml/2 tsp finely chopped fresh root ginger

10 ml/2 tsp chilli sauce

Salt and freshly ground black pepper

I like to cook the chicken with its skin on (for best flavour) but you can remove it before cooking if you prefer.

❶

Heat the oil in a frying pan (skillet) and brown the chicken portions on all sides. Transfer to the slo-cooker.

❷

Add the onion and celery to the pan and cook for about 5 minutes, stirring occasionally, without browning.

❸

Stir in the flour, then gradually stir in the stock. Add the pineapple and its juice and the remaining ingredients. Bring to the boil, stirring continuously. Pour over the chicken.

❹

Cover and cook on LOW for 5–8 hours.

Cooking time
5–8 hours on LOW

Moroccan chicken

15 ml/1 tbsp oil

1 onion, thinly sliced

1 garlic clove, crushed

2 carrots, thinly sliced

5 ml/1 tsp salt

2.5 ml/½ tsp ground turmeric

2.5 ml/½ tsp ground cinnamon

2.5 ml/½ tsp ground ginger

2.5 ml/½ tsp ground black pepper

425 g/15 oz/1 large can of
    chickpeas (garbanzos), drained

350 g/12 oz sweet potatoes, cut
    into cubes

450 ml/¾ pt/2 cups chicken stock

Finely grated rind of 1 lemon

15 ml/1 tbsp lemon juice

8 chicken thighs, skinned

*Serve this with heaps of fluffy couscous, perhaps with
some chopped fresh mint stirred into it.*

Heat the oil in a large saucepan, add the onion
and garlic and cook for about 5 minutes, stirring
occasionally, until beginning to turn golden brown.

Stir in the carrots, then the salt, turmeric,
cinnamon, ginger and pepper. Add the chickpeas,
sweet potatoes, stock and lemon rind. Bring just to
the boil and transfer to the slo-cooker.

Arrange the chicken on top of the vegetables,
pushing them gently into the liquid.

Cover and cook on LOW for 6–8 hours. Stir in
the lemon juice just before serving.

Cooking time
6–8 hours on LOW

Coq au vin

40 g/1½ oz/3 tbsp butter or margarine

4 chicken portions, skinned

2 onions, finely chopped

1 garlic clove, crushed

4 lean streaky bacon rashers (slices), rinded and finely chopped

100 g/4 oz button mushrooms, halved

50 g/2 oz/½ cup plain (all-purpose) flour

150 ml/¼ pt/⅔ cup chicken stock

300 ml/½ pt/1¼ cups red wine

2 bay leaves

1 bouquet garni (sachet)

Salt and freshly ground black pepper

This French dish is traditionally garnished with croûtons. I like to accompany it with baby (pearl) onions, cooked in a little butter and oil until golden brown and meltingly soft.

Heat the butter or margarine in a frying pan (skillet) and brown the chicken pieces on all sides. Transfer to the slo-cooker.

Add the onions, garlic and bacon to the pan and cook for about 8 minutes, stirring occasionally, until just beginning to turn golden brown.

Stir in the mushrooms and the flour, then gradually add the stock and wine, stirring all the time. Add the bay leaves and bouquet garni and season with salt and pepper. Bring to the boil and pour over the chicken in the slo-cooker.

Cover and cook on LOW for 6–8 hours.

Before serving, discard the bay leaves and bouquet garni and adjust the seasoning to taste.

Cooking time
6–8 hours on LOW

Chicken curry

30 ml/2 tbsp oil

8 chicken thighs, skinned and boned

Salt and freshly ground black pepper

1 onion, finely chopped

1 garlic clove, crushed

45 ml/3 tbsp sultanas (golden raisins)

30 ml/2 tbsp curry paste

30 ml/2 tbsp plain (all-purpose) flour

150 ml/¼ pt/⅔ cup chicken stock

This is good served with naan bread and spicy Indian chutneys.

1

Heat the oil in a frying pan (skillet) and lightly brown the chicken on all sides. Remove from the pan with a slotted spoon, place in the slo-cooker and season with salt and pepper.

2

Add the onion and garlic to the pan and cook for about 5 minutes, stirring occasionally, without browning.

3

Stir in the sultanas, curry paste and flour, then gradually stir in the stock. Bring to the boil, stirring, and pour into the slo-cooker.

4

Cover and cook on LOW for 6–8 hours.

Cooking time
6–8 hours on LOW

Buttered chicken with garlic

1 lemon, cut into quarters

4 garlic cloves

1.75 kg/4 lb chicken

60 ml/4 tbsp olive oil

100 g/4 oz/½ cup butter

45 ml/3 tbsp chopped fresh parsley

60 ml/4 tbsp dry white vermouth

This is a favourite in my family – they just love all the buttery juices spooned over the chicken. It's particularly good with roast potatoes and green beans. Use the recipe as a guide and buy a chicken that will fit into your slo-cooker.

1

Push the lemon pieces and one of the garlic cloves into the cavity of the chicken. Cut the remaining garlic into slivers.

2

Heat the oil and butter in a large frying pan (skillet) and quickly brown the chicken on all sides. Transfer to the slo-cooker.

3

Stir the garlic slivers, parsley and vermouth into the remaining butter in the saucepan, then pour over the chicken, scraping out every last drop.

4

Cover and cook on HIGH for 4–5 hours.

Cooking time
4–5 hours on HIGH

Chicken and tarragon

8 boneless chicken thighs, skinned

30 ml/2 tbsp oil

2 onions, finely chopped

1 garlic clove, crushed

2 lean streaky bacon rashers (slices), rinded and finely chopped

2 carrots, sliced

2 celery sticks, chopped

30 ml/2 tbsp plain (all-purpose) flour

450 ml/¾ pt/2 cups chicken stock

30 ml/2 tbsp tomato purée (paste)

30 ml/2 tbsp chopped fresh tarragon, plus extra to garnish

Salt and freshly ground black pepper

100 g/4 oz/1 cup frozen sweetcorn (corn)

1 red (bell) pepper, cut into small dice

Tarragon adds a wonderful flavour to chicken. If you can't get the fresh herb, use about 10 ml/2 tsp dried tarragon instead.

1

Cut each of the chicken pieces into two or three pieces.

2

Heat the oil in a frying pan (skillet) and quickly brown the chicken. Transfer to the slo-cooker.

3

Add the onions, garlic, bacon, carrots and celery to the pan and cook for 5 minutes, stirring occasionally, without browning.

4

Stir in the flour, then gradually stir in the stock and tomato purée. Add the tarragon and season with salt and pepper. Bring to the boil, stirring continuously. Pour over the chicken in the slo-cooker.

5

Cover and cook on LOW for 6–8 hours.

6

About 30 minutes to 1 hour before serving, stir in the sweetcorn and peppers.

7

Serve sprinkled with extra chopped tarragon.

Cooking time
6–8 hours on LOW

Chicken with mustard cream sauce SERVES 4

4 skinless chicken breasts

1 garlic clove, cut into slivers

Finely grated rind and juice of
   1 lemon

Salt and freshly ground black
   pepper

15 ml/1 tbsp olive oil

15 g/½ oz/1 tbsp butter or
   margarine

15 ml/1 tbsp clear honey

15 ml/1 tbsp wholegrain mustard

30 ml/2 tbsp double (heavy) cream

15 ml/1 tbsp chopped fresh parsley

*Serve with buttered tagliatelle and a salad of sliced
tomato and red onion.*

1

Make small cuts in the chicken breasts and
insert slivers of garlic and a little lemon rind. Season
the breasts with salt and pepper.

2

Heat the oil and butter or margarine in a frying
pan (skillet) and brown the chicken breasts quickly
on all sides. Lift from the saucepan into the
slo-cooker.

3

Stir the lemon juice and honey into the pan and
bring just to the boil. Pour the sauce over the
chicken, scraping out every last drop.

4

Cover and cook on LOW for 6–8 hours.

5

About 20 minutes before the end of the cooking
time, stir in the cream and parsley.

Cooking time
6–8 hours on LOW

Chicken rice with peppers

30 ml/2 tbsp oil

2 onions, finely chopped

225 g/8 oz chicken breast or thigh meat, cut into bite-size pieces

900 ml/1½ pts/3¾ cups chicken stock

1 small green (bell) pepper, chopped

1 small red (bell) pepper, chopped

100 g/4 oz button mushrooms

3 tomatoes, skinned and chopped

175 g/6 oz/¾ cup long-grain rice

50 g/2 oz/½ cup cooked ham, chopped

50 g/2 oz/¼ cup butter (optional)

Freshly grated Parmesan cheese

Serve this in shallow bowls with freshly grated or flaked Parmesan cheese scattered over the top.

1

Heat the oil in a large frying pan (skillet) and cook the onions for about 5 minutes, stirring occasionally, without browning. Add the chicken and cook for 2–3 minutes, stirring occasionally.

2

Add the stock and bring to the boil. Stir in all the remaining ingredients except the Parmesan and return just to the boil, then transfer to the slo-cooker.

3

Cover and cook on LOW for 3–4 hours.

4

Stir well, adding the butter, if using, and serve topped with Parmesan cheese.

Cooking time
3–4 hours on LOW

Duck with orange and spring onion SERVES 4

4 duck portions

1 onion, thinly sliced

1 orange

Salt and freshly ground black pepper

15 g/½ oz/1 tbsp butter or margarine

1 bunch of spring onions (scallions), chopped

15 ml/1 tbsp cornflour (cornstarch)

300 ml/½ pt/1¼ cups chicken stock

30 ml/2 tbsp marmalade

15 ml/1 tbsp light soy sauce

This is a great way to cook duck until it is meltingly tender. Serve it with new potatoes and fresh vegetables.

1

In a non-stick frying pan (skillet) cook the duck quickly, with no added fat, until the skin is deep golden brown.

2

Lay the onion slices in the base of the slo-cooker. Using a potato peeler or sharp knife, remove two or three strips of zest from the orange and add to the onions.

3

Arrange the duck on top and season with salt and pepper. Cover and cook on LOW for 4–8 hours.

4

Once the duck is cooked to your liking, squeeze the juice from the orange.

5

Melt the butter or margarine in a saucepan and cook the spring onions gently for 2 minutes, stirring occasionally.

6

Stir in the cornflour, then gradually stir in the stock. Add the orange juice, marmalade and soy sauce. Bring to the boil, stirring. Cover and keep warm.

7

Lift the duck out of the slo-cooker and keep warm.

8

Strain the contents of the slo-cooker into a bowl or 'skimmer' jug and allow to settle. Pour away the fat, leaving only the juices from the duck and onion. Stir this into the orange sauce.

9

Reheat the sauce and serve with the duck.

Cooking time
4–8 hours on LOW

Paella

30 ml/2 tbsp olive oil

1 onion, finely chopped

2 garlic cloves, crushed

225 g/8 oz chicken thigh meat, cut into small pieces

900 ml/1½ pts/3¾ cups chicken stock

A good pinch of saffron powder

225 g/8 oz/1 cup long-grain rice

4 tomatoes, skinned and chopped

1 red (bell) pepper, finely chopped

Salt and freshly ground black pepper

12 cooked mussels

12 cooked prawns (shrimp)

100 g/4 oz/1 cup frozen peas

Based on the classic Spanish dish, this version includes chicken, mussels and prawns.

1

Heat the oil in a large frying pan (skillet) and cook the onion and garlic for about 5 minutes, stirring occasionally, without browning.

2

Add the chicken and cook for 2–3 minutes, stirring occasionally.

3

Add the stock and saffron, bring to the boil, then stir in the rice, tomatoes and pepper. Season with salt and pepper. Return just to the boil and transfer to the slo-cooker.

4

Cover and cook on LOW for 3–4 hours.

5

About 30 minutes before serving, stir in the mussels, prawns and peas.

Cooking time
3–4 hours on LOW

Pot-roasted guinea fowl

4 whole cloves

½ lemon, cut into 4 pieces

1 oven-ready guinea fowl

25 g/1 oz/2 tbsp butter or
    margarine

3 leeks, sliced

1 carrot, cut into small dice

2 flat mushrooms, sliced

5 ml/1 tsp clear honey

150 ml/¼ pt/⅔ cup chicken stock or
    white wine

Salt and freshly ground black
    pepper

2 bacon rashers (slices), rinded

A few small sprigs of fresh herbs,
    such as thyme, rosemary and
    parsley

This is one of my husband's favourite recipes. Buy a bird that will sit comfortably inside the slo-cooker. Alternatively, it can be cut into joints.

1

Stick one clove into each lemon piece and slip them into the cavity of the guinea fowl.

2

Heat the butter in a large non-stick frying pan (skillet) and quickly brown the bird on all sides. Transfer to the slo-cooker.

3

Add the leeks, carrot, mushrooms and honey to the frying pan and cook for a few minutes, stirring occasionally, without browning. Add the stock and seasonings and bring to the boil.

4

Pour over the guinea fowl in the slo-cooker, spooning the vegetables over the breast area. Lay the bacon rashers and herbs over the top (this helps to keep the breast meat moist and adds flavour).

5

Cover and cook on HIGH for 3–4 hours.

Cooking time
3–4 hours on HIGH

Venison with red wine

900 g/2 lb stewing venison, cut into cubes

45 ml/3 tbsp olive oil

225 ml/8 fl oz/1 cup red wine

2 garlic cloves, very finely chopped

6 juniper berries

6 black peppercorns

4 cloves

1 cinnamon stick

½ lemon, cut into about 8 pieces

2 sprigs of fresh thyme

2 sprigs of fresh parsley

3 bacon rashers (slices), rinded and finely chopped

2 onions, chopped

1 carrot, thinly sliced

225 ml/8 fl oz/1 cup game or chicken stock

45 ml/3 tbsp redcurrant jelly (clear conserve)

Salt and freshly ground black pepper

Chopped fresh thyme and parsley, to serve

Venison is a lean meat that is ideal for slo-cooking. The venison is first marinated overnight in red wine and spices. I like to serve this with mashed potatoes and a green vegetable.

1

Put the venison into a large non-metallic bowl and add 15 ml/ 1 tbsp of the oil, the wine, cloves, juniper berries, peppercorns, cloves, cinnamon, lemon, thyme and parsley. Using clean hands, turn until well combined. Cover and leave to marinate in the fridge overnight, turning the meat occasionally if possible.

2

Using a slotted spoon, lift out the meat. Reserve the marinade but discard the thyme and parsley.

3

Heat 15 ml/1 tbsp of the remaining oil in a large non-stick frying pan (skillet) and brown the meat quickly (you may need to do this in batches) before transferring it to the slo-cooker.

4

Add the final 15 ml/1 tbsp oil to the frying pan and add the bacon. Cook quickly, stirring occasionally, until just beginning to turn golden brown.

5

Add the onions and carrot to the bacon and cook for a few minutes, stirring occasionally.

6

Stir in the reserved marinade (including all the bits and pieces), the stock, redcurrant jelly and seasoning. Bring to the boil and pour over the venison in the slo-cooker, coating it completely.

7

Cover and cook on LOW for 8–10 hours.

8

Before serving, remove the cinnamon stick, stir and adjust seasoning to taste.

9

Serve sprinkled with a little chopped fresh thyme and parsley.

Cooking time
8–10 hours on LOW

Pheasant in cider

30 ml/2 tbsp plain (all-purpose) flour

Salt and freshly ground black pepper

1 large pheasant, cut into joints if preferred

50 g/2 oz/¼ cup butter or margarine

1 onion, finely chopped

1 garlic clove, crushed

300 ml/½ pt/1¼ cups dry cider

1 bouquet garni (sachet)

4 lean streaky bacon rashers (slices), rinded

2 eating (dessert) apples

60 ml/4 tbsp soured (dairy-sour) cream

5 ml/1 tsp paprika

Make sure that you buy a pheasant that will fit easily into the slo-cooker. Otherwise, you will need to cut it into joints.

1

Season the flour with salt and pepper. Dust the pheasant in half the flour, shaking off any excess.

2

Heat half the butter or margarine in a large frying pan (skillet) and quickly brown the pheasant on all sides. Transfer to the slo-cooker.

3

Add the onion and garlic to the pan and cook for about 5 minutes, stirring occasionally, without browning.

4

Stir in the remaining flour and gradually stir in the cider. Bring to the boil, stirring. Add the bouquet garni and season with salt and pepper. Pour over the pheasant in the slo-cooker.

5

Cover and cook on HIGH for 3–4 hours.

6

Lift the pheasant from the slo-cooker, reserving the juices, cover with foil and keep warm.

7

Heat the remaining butter or margarine in a frying pan. Roll up the bacon rashers and fry (sauté) until crisp. Lift out and keep warm.

8

Peel, core and quarter the apples and add to the pan. Cook quickly until golden brown on both sides. Lift out and keep warm.

9

Strain the reserved cooking juices and reheat in a pan. Stir in the soured cream and paprika and heat until bubbling.

10

Serve the pheasant with the bacon rolls, apple wedges and sauce.

Cooking time
3–4 hours on HIGH

Turkey in fennel cream

30 ml/2 tbsp oil

450 g/1 lb turkey breast and/or
thigh meat, cut into cubes

1 onion, thinly sliced

1 small fennel bulb, sliced

2 carrots, chopped

30 ml/2 tbsp plain (all-purpose)
flour

300 ml/½ pt/1¼ cups chicken stock

5 ml/1 tsp dried mixed herbs

Salt and freshly ground black
pepper

150 ml/¼ pt/⅔ cup crème fraîche

*The fennel gives a lovely aniseed flavour to the sauce.
If you prefer, you could replace it with three sliced
celery sticks.*

1

Heat the oil in a frying pan (skillet) and cook
the turkey meat quickly until golden brown. With a
slotted spoon, transfer to the slo-cooker.

2

Add the onion, fennel and carrots to the pan
and cook for about 8 minutes, stirring occasionally,
without browning.

3

Stir in the flour, then gradually stir in the
stock. Bring to the boil, add the herbs and season
with salt and pepper. Pour over the turkey in the
slo-cooker.

4

Cover and cook on LOW for 6–8 hours.

5

About 30 minutes before serving, stir in the
crème fraîche and adjust the seasoning to taste.

Cooking time
6–8 hours on LOW

Puddings and Desserts

Everyone loves nursery puddings with lashings of custard and they cook superbly in the slo-cooker. If you need proof, just try the Maple Syrup Sponge Pudding on page 121 or Lemon Sponge on page 122.

The slo-cooker also excels in cooking fresh or dried fruit (the gentle cooking keeps it beautifully whole) and in simmering delicate desserts that normally require gentle heat, such as Baked Egg Custard (see page 127) and Crème Caramel (see page 126).

It's also wonderful for Christmas Pudding (see page 124). Having already cooked the pudding in the slo-cooker, you can pop it back in to reheat gently, with no attention needed, while you concentrate on preparing the rest of the Christmas dinner.

Quick tips for steamed puddings

- Preheat the slo-cooker on HIGH for 20 minutes while you make the pudding.
- Fill the bowl two-thirds full, to allow room for the pudding to rise.
- Cover the bowl tightly with buttered greaseproof (waxed) paper, tied on with string, or foil, crimped securely in place.
- Stand the bowl in the warmed slo-cooker.
- Pour round enough boiling water to come halfway up the sides of the bowl.
- Cook on HIGH for 3–4 hours only. After this, the pudding is likely to overcook.
- Make a foil handle to help lift the pudding in and out of the slo-cooker. Simply fold a thick strip of foil and place it underneath the basin, folding and securing it over the top.

Quick tips for fruit

- Prepare fresh fruit as normal, peeling and cutting or leaving it whole. Put it into the slo-cooker. Cover with a light sugar syrup (boiling water stirred with sugar to taste) – the fruit cooks more evenly if it is just immersed in the liquid. Cooking times will vary according the type and ripeness of the fruit. Here is a guide:

Orchard fruits, whole	LOW 5–10 hours
Orchard fruits, sliced	LOW 3–5 hours
Berry fruits	LOW 2–5 hours

- Dried fruit, such as apricots, figs, pears and apple rings, should also be immersed in liquid, to help them to plump up evenly. Cook them on LOW (or HIGH if you are in a hurry). Ready-to-eat varieties take less time to cook (about 4–6 hours) than standard dried fruit (about 6–10 hours).

Creamy rice pudding with nutmeg

25 g/1 oz/2 tbsp butter or margarine

900 ml/1½ pts/3¾ cups milk

150 ml/¼ pt/⅔ cup evaporated milk

100 g/4 oz/⅔ cup round-grain (pudding) rice

50 g/2 oz/¼ cup caster (superfine) sugar

2.5 ml/½ tsp vanilla essence (extract)

2.5 ml/½ tsp freshly grated nutmeg

Serve the pudding hot or at room temperature with crisp biscuits (cookies) to accompany it.

1

Grease the inside of the slo-cooker with butter or margarine.

2

Place all the ingredients into the slo-cooker and mix well. Dot with any remaining butter or margarine.

3

Cover and cook on LOW for 6–8 hours, stirring once or twice during the final 2 hours, if possible.

Cooking time
6–8 hours on LOW

Rhubarb and almond sponge pudding SERVES 4

100 g/4 oz/½ cup soft butter or margarine, plus extra for greasing

450 g/1 lb rhubarb, cut into 2.5 cm/1 in pieces

45 ml/3 tbsp caster (superfine) sugar

100 g/4 oz/½ cup soft brown sugar

2 eggs, beaten

10 ml/2 tsp almond essence (extract)

175 g/6 oz/1½ cups self-raising (self-rising) flour

15 ml/1 tbsp cocoa (unsweetened chocolate) powder

2.5 ml/½ tsp freshly grated nutmeg

This pudding is cooked and served in the cooking pot. Serve it with whipped cream, thick yoghurt or custard.

1

Lightly grease the inside of the slo-cooker, then preheat on HIGH while you prepare the pudding.

2

Arrange the rhubarb in the slo-cooker and sprinkle with the caster sugar.

3

Beat together the butter or margarine and brown sugar until light and fluffy. Gradually beat in the eggs and almond essence. Sift over the flour, cocoa and nutmeg and fold in with a metal spoon.

4

Spoon the mixture over the rhubarb and cover gently with a piece of greased greaseproof (waxed) paper, greased-side down.

5

Cover and cook on HIGH for 3–4 hours.

Cooking time
3–4 hours on HIGH

Apricot brioche and butter pudding

Butter or margarine, for greasing

6 slices of buttered brioche

75 g/3 oz/½ cup ready-to-eat dried apricots, chopped

30 ml/2 tbsp caster (superfine) sugar

3 eggs, beaten

A few drops of vanilla essence (extract)

450 ml/¾ pt/2 cups milk

Of course, you can use ordinary bread and sultanas or raisins for this recipe to make a traditional bread and butter pudding, or use fruit bread with other dried fruit such as chopped dates. Serve the pudding hot or at room temperature, as you prefer.

1

Grease an ovenproof dish that will fit into your slo-cooker. Cut the brioche into small triangles and arrange in the dish, scattering the apricots between the layers and over the top.

2

Lightly whisk together the sugar, eggs and vanilla essence.

3

Heat the milk until hot but not boiling, and pour on to the egg mixture, stirring well. Strain over the brioche.

4

Cover the dish securely with greased foil. Stand it in the slo-cooker and pour round sufficient boiling water to come halfway up the sides of the dish.

5

Cover and cook on LOW for 4–6 hours.

Cooking time
4–6 hours on LOW

Gingered rhubarb with orange SERVES 4

450 g/1 lb rhubarb, trimmed and
cut into 2.5 cm/1 in lengths

60 ml/4 tbsp caster (superfine)
sugar

30 ml/2 tbsp stem ginger syrup

Grated rind and juice of 1 orange

2 pieces of stem ginger in syrup,
drained and thinly sliced

*In the slo-cooker, the rhubarb stays beautifully whole.
Serve this warm or chilled with cream, yoghurt or custard.*

1

Toss the rhubarb in the sugar and put into the
slo-cooker.

2

Combine the ginger syrup with the orange rind
and juice and 150 ml/¼ pt/⅔ cup water. Pour over
the rhubarb.

3

Cover and cook on LOW for 4–6 hours.

4

Gently stir in the ginger slices and leave to cool
before serving.

Cooking time
4–6 hours on LOW

Above left **Coq au Vin** *(page 100)*

Left **Greek Mushrooms** *(page 47)*

Above **Duck with Orange and Spring Onion** *(page 106)*

Above **Maple Syrup Sponge Pudding** *(page 121)*
        Crème Caramel *(page 126)*
        Spiced Dried Fruit Salad *(page 133)*

Above right **Pears in Red Wine** *(page 132)*

Right **Spiced Dried Fruit Salad** *(page 133)*

Below **Gingered Rhubarb with Orange** *(page 120)*

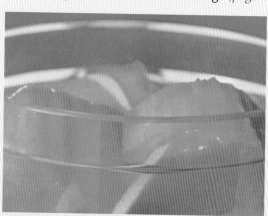

Maple syrup sponge pudding

60 ml/4 tbsp maple syrup

100 g/4 oz/½ cup soft butter or margarine, plus extra for greasing

100 g/4 oz/½ cup caster (superfine) sugar

2 eggs, lightly beaten

A few drops of vanilla essence (extract)

175 g/6 oz/1½ cups self-raising (self-rising) flour

30 ml/2 tbsp milk

Sponge puddings are everyone's favourite comfort pudding! You can, of course, use this recipe with ordinary golden (light corn) syrup, or replace the syrup with marmalade or jam (conserve).

1

Preheat the slo-cooker on HIGH while you make the pudding.

2

Grease a 1.2 litre/2 pt/5 cup pudding basin and spoon the syrup into the bottom.

3

In a large bowl, beat the butter or margarine and sugar together until light and fluffy. Gradually beat in the eggs and vanilla. Sift the flour over and, with a metal spoon, fold in with the milk.

4

Spoon the mixture on top of the syrup and level the top. Cover securely with buttered foil.

5

Put the basin in the slo-cooker and pour round sufficient boiling water to come halfway up the sides of the basin.

6

Cover and cook on HIGH for 3½–4½ hours.

7

Lift the pudding out and turn out on to a warm serving plate.

Cooking time
3½–4½ hours on HIGH

Lemon sponge

75 g/3 oz/⅓ cup soft butter or
margarine, plus extra for
greasing

100 g/4 oz/½ cup light muscovado
sugar

Finely grated rind of 1 lemon

1 large egg, lightly beaten

50 g/2 oz/½ cup self-raising (self-
rising) flour

2.5 ml/½ tsp baking powder

2.5 ml/½ tsp ground cinnamon

50 g/2 oz/½ cup porridge oats

15 ml/1 tbsp lemon juice

15–30 ml/1–2 tbsp milk

*The oats give this pudding a light, crumbly texture. Serve
it with lashings of custard.*

1

Preheat the slo-cooker on HIGH while you make
the pudding.

2

Lightly grease a 600 ml/1 pt/2½ cup pudding
basin and put a small disc of non-stick paper in the
bottom.

3

Beat the butter or margarine, sugar and lemon
rind until light and fluffy. Gradually beat in the
egg. Sift the flour, baking powder and cinnamon
over the top and add the oats. Fold in with a metal
spoon, adding the lemon juice and sufficient milk
to make a soft, dropping consistency.

4

Spoon into the prepared dish and cover securely
with buttered foil.

5

Stand the bowl in the warm slo-cooker and
pour round sufficient water to come halfway up
the sides.

6

Cover and cook on HIGH for 3–4 hours.

Cooking time
3–4 hours on HIGH

Baked stuffed apples

4 cooking (tart) apples

30 ml/2 tbsp raisins

30 ml/2 tbsp sultanas (golden raisins)

50 g/2 oz/½ cup soft brown sugar

15 ml/1 tbsp toasted hazelnuts (filberts)

2.5 ml/½ tsp ground cinnamon

Serve this old-fashioned favourite with plenty of creamy custard. My favourite fruit and nut combination is probably dates and toasted pine nuts.

1

Core the apples and peel off a thin strip around the 'equator' of each apple.

2

Mix together the raisins, sultanas, sugar, hazelnuts and cinnamon and press into the apple centres, piling any extra on top.

3

Stand the apples in the slo-cooker and add 60–75 ml/4–5 tbsp water.

4

Cover and cook on LOW for 3–6 hours.

Cooking time
3–6 hours on LOW

Christmas pudding

50 g/2 oz/½ cup plain (all-purpose) flour

5 ml/1 tsp ground mixed (apple-pie) spice

100 g/4 oz/2 cups fresh white breadcrumbs

150 g/5 oz/1¼ cups shredded (chopped) suet

100 g/4 oz/½ cup soft brown sugar

400 g/14 oz/2⅓ cups mixed dried fruit (fruit cake mix)

50 g/2 oz/⅓ cup chopped blanched almonds

1 small carrot, finely grated

Finely grated rind and juice of 1 orange

2 eggs, beaten

Christmas pudding is ideal for slo-cooking – just pop it in to cook all day or overnight. It can be reheated on Christmas day in the slo-cooker, away from the hustle and bustle of the oven and hob.

1

Preheat the slo-cooker on HIGH while you make the pudding.

2

Sift the flour and spice into a large bowl and mix in the breadcrumbs, suet, sugar, fruit, nuts, carrot and orange rind.

3

Whisk together the orange juice, eggs, treacle, brandy and beer or milk. Add to the bowl and mix together well.

4

Spoon the mixture into a greased 1.2 litre/2 pt/ 5 cup pudding basin and level the top. Cover securely with greased foil.

5

Stand the basin in the slo-cooker and pour round sufficient water to come three-quarters of the way up the sides of the basin.

6

Cover and cook on HIGH for 10–12 hours.

7

Remove from the slo-cooker, leave to cool completely, wrap in more foil and store in a cool, dark place.

15 ml/1 tbsp black treacle
  (molasses)

15 ml/1 tbsp brandy or dry sherry

75 ml/5 tbsp beer or milk

Butter or margarine, for greasing

8

To reheat, preheat the slo-cooker on HIGH for 20 minutes. Stand the pudding in the slo-cooker and pour round sufficient water to come three-quarters of the way up the sides of the basin. Cover and cook on LOW for about 8 hours, or on HIGH for about 4 hours.

Cooking time
10–12 hours on HIGH

Reheating time
8 hours on LOW or 4 hours on HIGH

Crème caramel

100 g/4 oz/½ cup caster (superfine) sugar

150 ml/¼ pt/⅔ cup water

Butter or margarine, for greasing

4 eggs

2.5 ml/½ tsp vanilla essence (extract)

300 ml/½ pt/1¼ cups milk

300 ml/½ pt/1¼ cups double (heavy) cream

A creamy custard topped with rich caramel. Serve it chilled.

1

First make the caramel: in a small saucepan, heat 30 ml/2 tbsp of the sugar with the water until the sugar has dissolved. Bring to the boil, then boil rapidly (watching it carefully so that it does not burn) until it turns golden brown. Pour into a buttered 18–20 cm/7–8 in ovenproof soufflé dish and swirl it over the base.

2

Lightly whisk together the eggs, vanilla essence and remaining sugar. Put the milk and cream into a saucepan and heat until hot but not boiling, and pour on to the egg mixture, stirring well. Strain the mixture over the caramel.

3

Cover the dish securely with foil, then stand it in the slo-cooker and pour round sufficient boiling water to come halfway up the sides of the dish.

4

Cover and cook on LOW for 3½–4½ hours until set (a knife inserted in the centre should come out clean if it is cooked).

5

Remove from the slo-cooker, leave to cool, then chill for several hours. Just before serving, gently ease the custard away from the sides of the dish and carefully turn out on to a serving dish.

Cooking time
3½–4½ hours on LOW

Baked egg custard

4 eggs

50 g/2 oz/¼ cup caster (superfine)
sugar

600 ml/1 pt/2½ cups milk

2.5 ml/½ tsp vanilla essence
(extract)

Butter or margarine, for greasing

Freshly grated nutmeg

*Serve this warm or chilled, either plain or with fresh soft
fruit or some chilled Spiced Dried Fruit Salad
(see page 133).*

1

Lightly whisk the eggs and sugar.

2

Heat the milk until hot but not boiling and
pour on to the egg mixture, stirring well. Add the
vanilla essence.

3

Strain the custard into a greased 18–20 cm/
7–8 in ovenproof soufflé dish. Sprinkle a little
grated nutmeg over the top, then cover securely
with foil.

4

Stand the dish in the slo-cooker and pour round
sufficient boiling water to come halfway up the
sides of the dish.

5

Cook on LOW for 3½–4½ hours until set (a knife
inserted in the centre should come out clean).

Cooking time
3½–4½ hours on LOW

Banana tea bread

175 g/6 oz/1½ cups self-raising (self-rising) flour

2.5 ml/½ tsp freshly grated nutmeg

75 g/3 oz/⅓ cup butter or margarine, plus extra for greasing

100 g/4 oz/½ cup soft brown sugar

50 g/2 oz/⅓ cup sultanas (golden raisins)

50 g/2 oz/⅓ cup chopped walnuts or pecan nuts

3 really ripe bananas, mashed

2 eggs, beaten

This is lovely served warm or cold, sliced and spread with butter. Great with a cup of tea!

1

Preheat the slo-cooker on HIGH while you make the cake.

2

Sift the flour and nutmeg into a large bowl and rub in the butter or margarine until the mixture resembles fine breadcrumbs. Stir in the sugar, sultanas and nuts.

3

Stir the bananas into the eggs and stir into the dry ingredients, mixing well.

4

Spoon the mixture into a buttered 18 cm/7 in cake tin (pan) and cover securely with greased foil. Stand the tin in the slo-cooker and pour round sufficient boiling water to come halfway up the sides of the tin.

5

Cover and cook on HIGH for 2–3 hours.

6

Lift the tin out of the slo-cooker and leave to stand for 10 minutes before turning out and cooling completely on a wire rack.

Cooking time
2–3 hours on HIGH

Gingerbread

225 g/8 oz/1 cup dark Muscovado sugar

175 g/6 oz/⅔ cup butter or margarine, plus extra for greasing

350 g/12 oz/1 cup golden (light corn) syrup

450 g/1 lb/4 cups plain (all-purpose) flour

5 ml/1 tsp salt

15 ml/1 tbsp ground ginger

10 ml/2 tsp baking powder

1 egg, beaten

300 ml/½ pt/1¼ cups milk

50 g/2 oz/⅓ cup glacé (candied) cherries, chopped

50 g/2 oz/¼ cup caster (superfine) sugar (optional)

Serve this warm as a pudding with custard or cold as a cake.

1

Preheat the slo-cooker on HIGH while you make the mixture.

2

Put the Muscovado sugar into a non-stick saucepan with the butter or margarine and syrup. Heat gently until the sugar has dissolved. Leave to cool slightly.

3

Sift the flour, salt, ginger and baking powder into a large bowl and make a well in the centre. Pour in the melted mixture and the egg and beat until smooth.

4

Pour into a greased 18 cm/7 in round cake tin (pan) and sprinkle with the cherries. Cover securely with greased foil and stand the tin in the slo-cooker. Pour round sufficient boiling water to come halfway up the sides of the tin. Cover and cook on HIGH for 5–7 hours or until set – a skewer inserted in the centre should come out clean.

5

Lift the tin out of the slo-cooker and leave to stand for 5 minutes before turning out.

6

If serving as a cake, mix the caster sugar with 30 ml/2 tbsp water and brush over the top of the hot gingerbread. Leave to cool completely.

Cooking time
5–7 hours on HIGH

Pineapple upside-down sponge

For the topping:

50 g/2 oz/¼ cup butter

100 g/4 oz/⅔ cup soft brown sugar

425 g/15 oz/1 large can of
pineapple rings in fruit juice,
drained

A few glacé (candied) cherries

For the sponge:

175 g/6 oz/⅔ cup soft butter or
margarine

175 g/6 oz/⅔ cup caster
(superfine) sugar

5 ml/1 tsp almond essence
(extract)

3 eggs, beaten

175 g/6 oz/1½ cups self-raising
(self-rising) flour

30 ml/2 tbsp milk

*You need to be available to turn the heat setting down
after the first hour. The sponge is cooked directly in the
slo-cooker pot and turned out for serving. Serve it warm
as pudding with crème fraîche or thick yoghurt,
or cold as a cake.*

Preheat the slo-cooker on HIGH.

For the topping, put the butter in the slo-cooker
to melt while it is preheating. Stir in the sugar, then
arrange the pineapple rings, with the cherries in the
centres, over the base of the pot.

To make the sponge, beat together the butter or
margarine, sugar and almond essence. Gradually
beat in the eggs, a little at a time.

Sift the flour over the top and fold in, with a
metal spoon, adding enough of the milk to make a
soft, dropping consistency. Spoon the mixture over
the pineapple.

Cover and cook on HIGH for 1 hour, then
switch to LOW for 2½–3½ hours.

Cooking time
1 hour on HIGH, then 2½–3½ hours on LOW

Chocolate sponge

For the sponge:

15 ml/1 tbsp cocoa (unsweetened chocolate) powder

100 g/4 oz/½ cup soft butter or margarine, plus extra for greasing

100 g/4 oz/½ cup caster (superfine) sugar

2 eggs, beaten

100 g/4 oz/1 cup self-raising (self-rising) flour, sifted

For the icing (frosting):

30 ml/2 tbsp cocoa (unsweetened chocolate) powder

225 g/8 oz/1⅓ cups icing (confectioners') sugar, sifted

75 g/3 oz/⅓ cup soft butter

45 ml/3 tbsp milk

1
Preheat the slo-cooker on HIGH while you make the cake.

2
To make the sponge, blend the cocoa to a paste with 30 ml/2 tbsp hot water. Beat the butter or margarine and sugar until light.

3
Beat in the cocoa mixture, then beat in the eggs, a little at a time and alternating with a little of the flour. With a metal spoon, gently fold in the remaining flour.

4
Spoon the mixture into a buttered 18 cm/7 in cake tin (pan) and cover securely with greased foil. Stand the tin in the slo-cooker and pour round sufficient boiling water to come halfway up the sides of the tin. Cover and cook on HIGH for 3–4 hours.

5
Lift the tin from the slo-cooker and leave to stand for 5 minutes before turning it out to cool.

6
To make the icing, blend the cocoa with 30 ml/ 2 tbsp hot water to make a paste. Gradually beat mixture into the butter, adding enough of the milk to make a smooth but fairly stiff icing.

7
Cut the cooled sponge in half horizontally, then sandwich together with half the icing. Spread the remaining icing on top.

Cooking time
3–4 hours on HIGH

Pears in red wine

600 ml/1 pt/2½ cups red wine

175 g/6 oz/¾ cup caster (superfine) sugar

Finely grated rind and juice of 1 lemon

2 whole cloves

1 cinnamon stick

4–6 firm pears, peeled and left whole

I like to serve these pears chilled with a dollop of really thick double (heavy) or clotted cream (indulgent, but delicious!).

1
Put the wine, sugar, lemon rind and juice and cloves into the slo-cooker and stir.

2
Cut a small slice off the bottom of each pear so that they will stand upright. Stand them in the wine, then add sufficient boiling water to come almost to the top of the pears.

3
Cover and cook on LOW for 6–10 hours until the pears are very tender.

4
Lift the pears out of the liquid and put them in a bowl. Tip the wine mixture into a saucepan, bring to the boil and bubble until it has reduced by about two-thirds and thickened.

5
Pour over the pears and leave to cool completely before serving.

Cooking time
6–10 hours on LOW

Spiced dried fruit salad

225 g/8 oz/1⅓ cups mixed dried
  fruit, such as apricots, prunes,
  figs, peaches, pears and apple
  rings

30 ml/2 tbsp soft brown sugar
  (optional)

600 ml/1 pt/2½ cups apple juice

1 cinnamon stick

4 whole cloves

Thinly sliced zest of 1 lemon or
  orange

Dried fruit plumps up and softens beautifully in the slo-cooker. You can vary the fruits and spices used to suit your own taste and instead of apple juice, try cider or wine. Serve it warm or chilled for breakfast or as a dessert with thick yoghurt or cream.

1
Put the fruit into the slo-cooker and sprinkle over the sugar, if using. Pour the apple juice over and add the spices and zest.

2
Cover and cook on LOW for 6–10 hours (ready-to-eat dried fruit will soften more quickly than the ordinary dried varieties).

Cooking time
6–10 hours on LOW

Figs in orange and green ginger wine

450 g/1 lb dried figs (not the ready-to-eat variety)

450 ml/¾ pt/2 cups orange juice

300 ml/½ pt/1¼ cups green ginger wine

15–30 ml/1–2 tbsp fresh lemon juice

Chopped pistachio nuts, to serve

This rich-tasting dessert can be served either warm with ice cream or chilled with thick Greek yoghurt. There is lots of juice which, if you like, can be brought to the boil in a saucepan on the hob and reduced to a thicker consistency.

1

Arrange the figs in an even layer in the slo-cooker. Pour over the orange juice and wine.

2

Cover and cook on AUTO for 9–11 hours, stirring once or twice during the second half of cooking if possible.

3

Before serving, stir in lemon juice to taste.

4

Serve warm or chilled, sprinkled with pistachio nuts.

Cooking time
9–11 hours on AUTO

Greek figs with Marsala

12 fresh figs

75 ml/5 tbsp clear honey

60 ml/4 tbsp Marsala wine

Juice of ½ lemon

A few sprigs of fresh thyme

Toasted flaked (slivered) almonds,
    to serve

Serve warm or chilled with thick Greek yoghurt.

1

Arrange the figs in the slo-cooker, packing them closely, in a single layer if possible.

2

Drizzle the honey and Marsala evenly over the figs. Sprinkle with the lemon juice and tuck in the thyme sprigs.

3

Cover and cook on AUTO for 5–7 hours until soft and tender.

4

Place the figs on serving plates and spoon the juices over. Serve warm or leave to cool and chill until needed. Sprinkle with toasted almonds just before bringing to the table.

Cooking time
5–7 hours on AUTO

Nutty chocolate fondue

200 g/7 oz plain (semi-sweet) chocolate

150 ml/¼ pt/⅔ cup single (light) cream

2.5 ml/½ tsp mixed (apple-pie) spice

45 ml/3 tbsp brandy, rum or orange liqueur

30 ml/2 tbsp chopped toasted nuts, such as hazelnuts or almonds

For dipping:

Fresh fruit, such as apple and pear wedges, orange segments, pineapple slices, chunks of mango, papaya and melon, lychees, physalis, etc.

Ready-to-eat dried fruits, such as apricots, figs and dates

Whole nuts, such as brazil nuts, walnuts, pecans and almonds

Sponge (lady) fingers and crisp biscuits

This is a delightful way to end a meal. Each person dips their own pieces of fresh fruit, nuts or biscuits (cookies) into the velvety chocolate.

1
Break the chocolate into the slo-cooker and heat on HIGH for about 30 minutes.

2
Turn the heat setting down to LOW and stir in the cream and spice. Cook on LOW for 1–1½ hours.

3
Just before serving, stir in the alcohol and nuts.

4
Take the slo-cooker pot to the table and get dipping!

Cooking time
30 minutes on HIGH and 1–1½ hours on LOW

The recipes in this section don't fit easily into any of the other chapters of this book but they show the full range of your slo-cooker's versatility. It is ideal for recipes that rely on slow, gentle cooking, like Lemon Curd and Cheese Fondue, and it makes perfect chunky Apple Chutney.

And at Hallowe'en, Bonfire Night or Christmas, why not heat your Mulled Wine in the slo-cooker?

Apple chutney

1.5 kg/3 lb apples, peeled, cored and chopped

450 g/1 lb onions, finely chopped

700 g/1½ lb/3½ cups soft brown sugar

225 g/8 oz/1⅓ cups sultanas (golden raisins)

300 ml/½ pt/1¼ cups wine vinegar

1 garlic clove, crushed

15 ml/1 tbsp salt

5 ml/2 tsp pickling spice, tied up in a muslin (cheese cloth) bag

A pinch of cayenne (optional)

①
Put all the ingredients into the slo-cooker and mix well.

②
Cover and cook on LOW for 10–12 hours, stirring once or twice during the second half of cooking if possible.

③
Remove the spice bag, spoon into sterilised jars, cool and seal.

Cooking time
10–12 hours on LOW

Lemon curd

100 g/4 oz/½ cup butter

Finely grated rind and juice of
    4 lemons

450 g/1 lb/2 cups caster
    (superfine) sugar

4 eggs, lightly beaten

There is nothing quite like the fresh taste of home-made lemon curd. Keep it in the fridge and use it within about 3 weeks (if you can resist it that long!).

❶

Melt the butter in a saucepan and add the lemon rind and juice and sugar. Heat gently, stirring, until the sugar dissolves. Leave to cool.

❷

Stir the eggs into the cooled mixture and strain into a 1.2 litre/2 pt/5 cup pudding basin or soufflé dish. Cover securely with foil and stand in the slo-cooker. Pour round sufficient water to come halfway up the sides of the basin.

❸

Cover and cook on LOW for 3–4½ hours until thick.

❹

Pour into sterilised jars, cool and seal. Store in the fridge for up to 3 weeks.

Cooking time
3–4½ hours on LOW

Cheese fondue

140

1 garlic clove, halved

225 g/8 oz/2 cups Gruyère (Swiss) or Gouda cheese, grated

225 g/8 oz/2 cups Emmenthal cheese, grated

15 ml/ 1 tbsp cornflour (cornstarch)

A pinch of white pepper

A pinch of freshly grated nutmeg

150 ml/¼ pt/⅔ cup dry white wine

The low setting of the slo-cooker is ideal for heating the cheeses gently so that they don't become rubbery. Serve cubes of crusty bread for dipping into the fondue.

1

Rub the inside of the slo-cooker with the cut sides of the garlic.

2

Combine the cheeses, cornflour, pepper and nutmeg and put into the slo-cooker. Add the wine.

3

Cover and cook on LOW for 2–3 hours, stirring occasionally.

Cooking time
2–3 hours on LOW

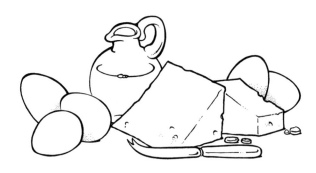

Mulled wine

2 bottles of red wine

1 lemon

1 orange, sliced

60 ml/4 tbsp sugar

2 cinnamon sticks

A pinch of ground cloves

A pinch of mixed (apple-pie) spice

60 ml/4 tbsp brandy (optional)

1
Preheat the slo-cooker on HIGH for 20 minutes.

2
Pour the wine into the warm slo-cooker. Using a potato peeler or sharp knife, remove the zest of the lemon in strips. Squeeze the juice from the lemon. Add zest and juice to the wine.

3
Add all the remaining ingredients, except the brandy.

4
Cover and cook on LOW for 2 hours.

5
Just before serving, stir in the brandy, if using.

Cooking time
2 hours on LOW

Index

apples
  apple chutney 138
  baked stuffed apples 123
apricot brioche and butter
  pudding 119

bacon
  and apple pudding 97
  cassoulet 96
  glazed bacon with red onions
  92
  liver and bacon casserole 86
  pot-roast bacon with apple 95
  Somerset bacon hot-pot 94
baked beans, spicy sausage, bean
  and potato 75
baked egg custard 127
baked stuffed apples 123
banana tea bread 128
beef
  bolognese sauce 72
  bourguignon 70
  in brown ale 74
  with herb dumplings 71
  Hungarian beef 65
  Italian-style beef in wine 66
  old-fashioned beef broth 21
  and orange casserole 67
  steak and ale pudding 73
  stroganoff 69
  sweet and sour 68
bolognese sauce 72
browning method 12, 13, 17
butter bean and tomato soup 22
buttered chicken with garlic 102
cassoulet 96
cheese fondue 140
cheese-stuffed onions 49

chicken
  buttered chicken with garlic 102
  cassoulet 96
  chowder 20
  coq au vin 100
  curry 101
  liver pâté 34–5
  Moroccan 99
  with mustard cream sauce 104
  paella 108
  rice with peppers 105
  spicy gingered chicken with
   pineapple 98
  and tarragon 103
  traditional mulligatawny
   soup 32
chickpeas
  curried chickpeas and okra 48
  Moroccan chicken 99
  spiced vegetables and
   barley 53
chilled cucumber and mint
  soup 31
chocolate
  nutty chocolate fondue 136
  sponge 131
Christmas pudding 124–5
coq au vin 100
courgettes
  in apple juice 45
  haddock and courgettes in
   wine 57
creamy rice pudding with
  nutmeg 117
crème caramel 126
cucumber, chilled cucumber and
  mint soup 31
curried chickpeas and okra 48

curried pork with pineapple 91
curry sauce 38

dried fruit
  Persian rice 52
  spiced dried fruit salad 133
duck with orange and spring
  onion 106–7

eggs
  baked egg custard 127
  crème caramel 126

farmhouse pâté 33
figs
  Greek figs with Marsala 135
  in orange and green ginger
   wine 134
fish
  cooking 55
  Italian fish 60
  see also individual types such as
   plaice
French onion soup 24
fresh tomato sauce 41
fresh tomato soup 26
frozen ingredients 12, 44
fruit, cooking 116

game *see* poultry and game
gingerbread 129
gingered rhubarb with
  orange 120
glazed bacon with red onions 92
Greek figs with Marsala 135
Greek mushrooms 47
guinea fowl, pot-roasted 109

haddock and courgettes in wine 57
haricot beans, cassoulet 96
herrings, rollmop 58
home-made stock 19
Hungarian beef 65

Italian fish 60
Italian-style beef in wine 66

kleftiko 78–9

lamb
 with garlic, rosemary and ginger 80
 with gremolada 81
 kleftiko 78–9
 leg of lamb with garlic and rosemary 84
 minted lamb in tomato sauce 85
 in mushroom sauce 82
 navarin of lamb 87
 and onions in a red wine sauce 83
lambs' liver 33
leeks
 leek and cider hotpot 51
 vichyssoise 30
leg of lamb with garlic and rosemary 84
lemon curd 139
lemon sponge 122
liver and bacon casserole 86

mackerel and monkfish bake 56
Malay spiced pork 93
maple syrup sponge pudding 121
meat
 cooking times 64

preparation 11–12, 63
 see also individual types such as beef
minted lamb in tomato sauce 85
monkfish, mackerel and monkfish bake 56
Moroccan chicken 99
mulled wine 141
mulligatawny soup, traditional 32
mushrooms
 Greek 47
 lamb in mushroom sauce 82
 mushroom sauce 40
 pork and mushroom casserole 90

navarin of lamb 87
nutty chocolate fondue 136

okra, curried chickpeas and 48
old-fashioned beef broth 21
one-step method 13–14
onions
 cheese-stuffed 49
 French onion soup 24
oxtail casserole with redcurrant jelly 76–7

paella 108
pâté
 chicken liver 34–5
 farmhouse 33
pears in red wine 132
Persian rice 52
pheasant in cider 112–13
pineapple upside-down sponge 130
plaice, stuffed plaice in orange sauce 59

pork 93
 in apple and cider sauce 89
 curried pork with pineapple 91
 Malay spiced pork 93
 and mushroom casserole 90
 sweet and sour pork chops 88
pot-roast bacon with apple 95
pot-roasted guinea fowl 109
poultry and game
 preparation 63
 see also individual types such as chicken
pulses 44
 butter bean and tomato soup 22
 cassoulet 96
 curried chickpeas and okra 48
 Moroccan chicken 99
 red lentil soup 27
 spiced lentil and coconut soup 25
 spiced vegetables and barley 53
 spicy sausage, bean and potato 75
 split pea soup 23

ratatouille 50
red lentils
 red lentil soup 27
 spiced lentil and coconut soup 25
red mullet, Italian fish 60
rhubarb
 and almond sponge pudding 118
 gingered rhubarb with orange 120
rice
 paella 108

Persian 52
  stuffed vine leaves 36
rice pudding, creamy rice
  pudding with nutmeg 117
rollmop herrings 58

sausages, spicy sausage, bean
  and potato 75
seafood, paella 108
seasoning 12, 44
skate in tomato and olive
  sauce 61
slo-cookers
  adapting recipes for 14
  cooking methods 13–14
  cooking times 10–11, 64
  heat settings 8, 10, 64
  precautions 10
  preparation of ingredients
    11–12
Somerset bacon hot-pot 94
soups, serving 18

Spanish sauce 37
spiced dried fruit salad 133
spiced lentil and coconut
  soup 25
spiced vegetables and barley 53
spicy gingered chicken with
  pineapple 98
spicy sausage, bean and
  potato 75
split pea soup 23
steak and ale pudding 73
steamed puddings 115
stock
  home-made 19
  for soups and sauces 18
stuffed plaice in orange sauce 59
stuffed vine leaves 36
sweet and sour beef 68
sweet and sour pork chops 88
sweet and sour sauce 39

thickening 12

tomatoes
  butter bean and tomato
    soup 22
  fresh tomato sauce 41
  fresh tomato soup 26
traditional mulligatawny
  soup 32
trout, Italian fish 60
turkey in fennel cream 114

vegetables
  cooking 43–4
  preparation 11, 12, 17, 43
venison with red wine 110–11
vichyssoise 30
vine leaves, stuffed 36

watercress soup 29
wine, mulled 141
winter vegetable soup 28
winter vegetables in coconut
  cream 46